SEATS OF LONDON

Andrew Martin's books have often had a railway theme.
He is the author of a series of historical thrillers featuring
the Edwardian railwayman, Jim Stringer, beginning with
The Necropolis Railway. His non-fiction railway books
include *Underground Overground* and *Night Trains*.
His latest novel is *The Winker*, which is set in Britain and
France in 1976, and concerns a man who winks at people and
then kills them. (A couple of train journeys are involved.)

jimstringernovels.com

SEATS OF LONDON

A FIELD GUIDE TO LONDON TRANSPORT MOQUETTE PATTERNS

Andrew Martin

First published 2019 by
Safe Haven Books Ltd
12 Chinnocks Wharf
42 Narrow Street
London E14 8DJ
www.safehavenbooks.co.uk

A catalogue record for this book is available from the
British Library.

ISBN 978 1 916045 31 6
10 9 8 7 6 5 4 3 2 1
2023 2022 2021 2020 2019

Typeset in Johnston 1^0 and designed by
TimPetersDesign.co.uk
Printed and bound in the EU by GraphyCems, Spain

Acknowledgements

The Publisher and Author would like to thank the following for their assistance during the research and production of this book: Georgia Morley, Chris Nix, David Simpson and Caroline Warhurst at the London Transport Museum, and Keith Raeburn and Debbie Barnes at its Acton Depot; Thomas Riggs at TfL Images; Hannah Bale at Crich Tramway Museum, Derbyshire; Ciara Crossan and colleagues at Camira Fabrics; Kate Walsh at Wallace Sewell; Alan Powers; Oliver Green; Ivan Bennett; Andrew and Stuart Wells; Melanie Sharp; David Welch for all the last-minute fractals work; and Sarah Bolton for the waistcoat. Special thanks go to Laura Mullins at the London Transport Museum and Nigel Fryatt, Curator at the London Bus Museum, Brooklands.

Picture credits

All pictures © TfL from the London Transport Museum Collection except:

9 (left), 10 (right), 18, 19, 136 (bottom), 137, Camira Fabrics
10 (left), Stuart Wells
25, Keith Rayburn
26-27, © Sarah Rathbone
30, 80-81, 96, Chris Nix
36, 42 (top), 43, 98-99, 108 (bottom), Nigel Fryatt
41, Hannah Bale
46 (right), 47 (right), 48, 56 (bottom), Lund Humphries
64 (bottom), © Peter Denton
65, Private Collection © Redfern Gallery, London/Bridgeman Images
100 (right), Roger Cox
102-3, © Menja Stevenson

108 (top), Bluebell Railway
120-1, David Holdsworth
19 (right), 136 (top), 148-9, 152 (bottom), 168, 169 (right), 176-7, 180-1, 184, 190 (left), Safe Haven Books
2-3, 138, 142 (bottom), 160 (bottom), 164, 166, 170, 172 (right), 182, 186 (top), 187, 188, © TfL Images
155, 156-7, 159, 173, 179 (top), 183, 185, 189, Wallace Sewell
160 (top), 191 (right), Alamy
172 (left), Katy Bluey Phoenix
174-5, 179 (bottom left), © Emilia Cocking
190 (right), 'AEC Southall'
191 (left), Redroutemaster

Further reading

Overground, Underground: A Passenger's History of the Tube by Andrew Martin (Profile, 2012)
Underground Movement by Paul Moss (Capital Transport, 2000)
Designed for London: 150 Years of Transport Design by Oliver Green and Jeremy Rewse-Davies (Laurence King, 1995)
The Bus We Loved: London's Affair with the Routemaster by Travis Elborough (Granta, 2005)
Enid Marx: The Pleasures of Pattern by Alan Powers (Lund Humphries, 2018)
Cutting Edge: Modernist British Printmaking (Philip Wilson Publishers, 2019)

Contents

Introduction

The indexes of most books on the Underground bound blithely from 'Moorgate' to 'Morden', with no mention of 'Moquette'. In the typical YouTube film about a historic bus, a curator standing next to the bonnet will eventually say, 'Now let's have a look inside', whereupon the lower deck, filmed from the rear, reveals merely the anonymous backs of the seats; never the colourfully patterned material we actually sit on.

But that, I suggest, is what most people retain from their trip on a bus or the Tube. Moquette is the madeleine of our journeys, the memory trigger.

Straub, for example, as the blue checked moquette found on Tubes and buses from the 1970s is called, takes me back to my early visits to London. As a boy, I travelled down from York alone using my 'privilege' ticket, because my dad worked on British Rail. I recall sitting on Straub with my dad's battered A-Z (it dated from the 1950s) clutched rather anxiously . . . in the smoking

carriages of Tubes because my dad – who smoked – advised me that 'smokers tend to be the nicest people'. I negotiated the city entirely by Tube – even from, say, Charing Cross to Leicester Square – because I didn't know the way by surface, and the public street maps had always been carefully vandalised over the legend 'You are here'.

Frank Pick, the design guru of London Transport, also grew up in York. Finding London sprawling and unknowable as a boy, subsequently Pick sought, through design, to make it comprehensible. Ultimately he felt he had failed, but he gave it a good go.

Pick devised the Underground roundel; he commissioned the Johnston typeface and the Tube Map, and he recruited the most progressive poster designers and architects. Nothing was too good for the ordinary, fare-paying Londoner. Look at Piccadilly Circus station, where there is a memorial to Pick: brass, hardwoods, marble; shops, public lavatories, and a clock for telling the time anywhere in the world, Piccadilly Circus,

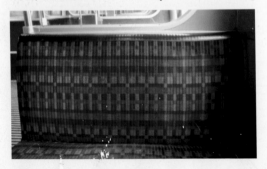

of course, being the centre *of* the world. And he commissioned some of the best moquettes.

That peerless tradition continues to this day. The pattern on the fabric covering the seat we sit on, from the Croydon Tramlink to the number

73, has been as carefully thought about as the vehicle itself. But hitherto moquette-creation, unlike Tube station architecture, seems to have been an unfairly overlooked art.

In writing this book I developed a strong affection for this underdog discipline. Indeed, I began to see potential moquettes everywhere. My second-favourite tie suddenly seemed to have moquette possibilities, as did my pyjamas, and several of my wife's dresses (and one of Theresa May's). To the consternation of fellow passengers I will rub my hand over the seat, trying to feel where the pile is cut or uncut (all will be explained). If the seat structure is 'grinning' through, to use the slightly macabre official term for 'worn', I might photograph it, giving the impression, perhaps, of being a man with an Imaginary Friend.

'The quality of our surroundings,' said Frank Pick, 'contributes to the quality of our own lives.' Here is a way of looking at moquette: it is traditional, very British, comfortable, warm, naturally fire-resistant (being wool), relatively expensive compared to other materials that might be put on seats, and frequently beautiful . . . and it has been made for *you*. From a hundred years of London's history, as many as possible are illustrated and discussed in this book.

RARITY RATING 🪑🪑🪑🪑🪑

This rating out of five is not a calibration of a moquette's merit or demerit: rather it denotes its ubiquity. Some of the moquettes depicted existed only as woven samples or even mere sketches, and never covered a single seat, so they get a zero rating, however beautiful they were.

Moquette: what is it and why is it used?

Moquette is French for carpet, and is best understood as *being* a lightweight carpet. Traditionally it was all wool with a cotton backing, but latterly nylon (say, 15 per cent) has been added

British wool and, if you really want to know, the most favoured donor is a Blue-faced Leicester crossed with a hill sheep. (The cross-breeding, of course, is to increase meat yield: wool is just a by-product, and a far from lucrative one.) These sheep are mostly to be found in the Scottish borders and around the Yorkshire Dales.

The photograph shows one that has just selflessly given up its coat on Andrew Wells's farm just over the border in Cumbria, released to speculate, back at pasture, whether it will have contributed to Barman on the Jubilee Line, or perhaps a heritage-train moquette like the one below, which originally appeared on *The Flying Scotsman*.

for extra resilience. It is a tufted fabric – in other words, it has a pile – with the tufts formed of a series of loops. To see an individual tuft or loop, look at where part of a pattern has been created by pixilation – say, around the circle representing the clock of Big Ben on the Barman moquette (see page 165). Each pixel is a tuft.

Sometimes the loops are cut, making them into fronds, and the fabric slightly weaker, ruling out pixilation – but then again, colours are more intense in areas of cut loop. A moquette might be all cut, all uncut, or a mixture.

These days London's moquette is woven from

The moquette on London's public transport is usually densely patterned, partly for decorative

effect, and partly to hide the dirt. A single colour (even all black) would soon look disgusting. Usually only four colours are involved for the sake of economy, but four might look like more depending on how they are matched. The moquettes are woven on jacquard looms, into which a complicated pattern can be programmed.

Moquette, like any sheep, is thermally efficient (relatively cool when it's hot and vice-versa) and fire-resistant. 'It's very hard to burn a hole in it with a cigarette,' one museum curator told me, and it appeared he had tried. The pile makes it more comfortable than a flat fabric, regardless of the upholstery beneath. Moquette also gives 'hold' – grips you in the seat, a useful property in central London where the Tube trains and buses tend to squirm about, following an essentially medieval street pattern.

Moquette has been the default option on London Tubes, buses and trams for a hundred years, and we are lucky to have it, because it is relatively expensive to create, install and maintain. Flat fabrics or plastic, for instance, would be much cheaper, and are often used abroad (see p. 136); they are also much uglier.

The new Underground trains due in 2023 will have moquette; so will Crossrail. The only thing likely to displace it would be the removal of seats themselves, which has been discussed as a way of increasing capacity on selected Tube carriages. But this is unlikely, because the longitudinal seats of today take up a space that could not be otherwise used. No full-grown person could stand up in it.

Exhibited at the London Transport Museum is a horse-drawn bus operated by the early fleet owner (and former bus driver), Thomas Tilling. It ran in London from about 1875 to 1895, and is a double-decker. In the lower deck, the seating has cushions covered with red material (not moquette); the original would have had something similar. The top deck, on the other hand, is exactly as it was. The top decks of early buses had no roof; or you could say the top-deck *was* the roof. Roofed-over top decks, it was thought – by the Metropolitan Police Public Carriage Office – would make them top-heavy, and liable to fall over.

Being open to the elements, these early top decks had wooden seats, initially (as here) a central longitudinal back-to-back bench known as a knifeboard, because it resembled a knife-cleaning board. It was no cheaper to sit on the roof than inside the bus, so naturally it was avoided in bad weather.

Buses were not for the hoi-polloi. The hoi-polloi walked. On the top deck would have been clerks rather than labourers. But the clerks might have been a bit frisky, so women tended to avoid the top deck, especially given the difficulty of climbing the ladder in long skirts. There was a modesty board at the side of the top deck to prevent pedestrians trying to look up those skirts.

GARDEN SEATS

To continue with open-topped buses . . .

People liked the top deck for the view, and some made the point of sitting next to the driver, enabling them to share his leather-covered transverse seat at the front. 'The old-fashioned bus driver', wrote the Reverend A. R. Buckland in 1892 in the magazine *Good Words*, 'is often a man with whom it is worth talking. He can enliven the monotony of a long drive by anecdotes not always, perhaps, veracious, but passing for truth in his own circle.'

In spite – or because of – the difficulty of climbing the previously-mentioned ladder, it was something of a feminist statement to travel on the top deck of a bus. Amy Levy's novel, *The Romance of a Shop*, describes Gertrude (one of four sisters who run a photographic shop on Baker Street) as 'careering up the street on the summit of a tall, green omnibus, her hair blowing gaily in the breeze.' The book was published in 1888. By then, the knifeboard had given way to slatted benches in a transverse arrangement. These were called 'garden seats', and they were usually accessed by spiral staircase, easier for women to climb than the old ladders. But it still meant sitting on bare wood, and not padded seats upholstered in moquette.

1890 STOCK

The City & South London Railway was the first deep-level Underground line. In other words, the first Tube, as opposed to the earlier sub-surface lines (Metropolitan and District) which were built in trenches that were then (usually) covered over again.

The C&SL ran from Stockwell to King William Street, and would eventually become part of the City branch of the Northern Line. It was powered by electricity, as all Tubes have to be. You can't run a steam train in a tunnel of 12-foot 2-inches diameter, which was the niggardly size of the C&SL tunnels. (They were later widened.) The line was also lit by electricity, 'perhaps almost enough', John Glover notes in *London's Underground*, 'to read a newspaper by" Continuing in this tone of faint praise, Glover adds that 'the tram alternative had oil lamps and negligible upholstery.'

But the C&SL carriages seemed to have too *much* upholstery. It ran right up the walls, leaving room for only tiny slits of windows. The effect was claustrophobic, hence the nickname 'padded cells' for these carriages, which had transverse seating, in which the genteel might be in a staring match with the riff-raff, there being only one class, an idea copied from the New York Elevated Railroad. (Like most of the early Tubes, the C&SLR was built with American capital.) Whether the upholstery was moquette is not known, even by the curators of the LT Museum, where one preserved C&SLR carriage is exhibited, with the seat covered in a kind of fawn velvet. One curator told me, 'We've kept it deliberately neutral, in the absence of hard information about the seats.' He

does suspect, though, that the original covering was faux-leather, or rexine, because we are still not quite in the moquette era.

The Oxford Companion to British Railway History said of the C&SLR, 'Everything was too small.' John Betjeman wrote that 'It smelled of feet,' and the carriages might have continued to smell of feet in their retirement, since they tended to become changing rooms on the boundaries of cricket pitches, their original seat covering gradually disintegrating and fading into historical obscurity.

AN EARLY MOQUETTE

The Metropolitan Railway began in 1863 as an underground railway using steam engines (hence, of course, very smoky and steamy tunnels). It was partly electrified from 1902, but the services to its country stations beyond Rickmansworth were steam-hauled until 1962. (It is depressing to think that I was alive, albeit only just, when this was going on.)

It is hard to generalise about moquette on the early Metropolitan: there were no photographs to begin with, and then there were only black-and-white ones. Also, the Met ran a great variety of trains: compartment stock, saloons, steam-hauled, electric-hauled, and electrical multiple units. And there were at first three classes of accommodation on the Met. (It went down to two in 1905, and one in 1941, by which time the Metropolitan Railway had been incorporated into LT as the Metropolitan Line).

Moreover, this railway was simultaneously an aspirant main line, a country branch and an Underground line. The country line – up to Amersham and Chesham – was finally electrified along its whole length in 1962, and some wooden

carriages dating from 1900, which had been used on the steam-hauled shuttle to Chesham, were therefore retired. Four were then bought by the Bluebell Railway for £65 each, which was far cheaper than the prices of ex-BR carriages.

In 1898, the *Engineer* magazine had previewed the seating in these carriages, which were composites, meaning more than one class. In third class, the seats were rep (a tough, corded fabric); in second class velvet, and in first class there was 'figured rose-coloured Baghdad moquette finished with silk lace and cord.'

The seat coverings changed many times thereafter, and the moquette pictured is believed to have featured on the carriages following a refit of 1925. I think this was an off-the-peg railway moquette. Something very similar is on a Midland Railway carriage at the National Railway Museum in York.

Another of the Bogie Stock coaches ended up in the LT Museum, where its compartments have been fitted with moquettes representative of the Metropolitan in 1900, the 1920s and 1950s.

Who makes London's moquette?

Currently the sole supplier of moquette to London Underground is Camira Fabrics, whose moquettes are also on many London buses. In 2007, Camira acquired Holdsworth and Co., then the chief supplier of moquette to LT (see pp. 120-1.)

Given that moquette is predominantly wool, Camira's head office is satisfyingly located in rolling West Yorkshire countryside near Huddersfield. I couldn't actually see any sheep as I drove by the bright green meadows, but I felt the sighting of a flock was imminent.

The Camira premises are airy and modern, but also barn-like with exposed wooden beams, and stand on the site of an old water-powered textile mill. The water wheel is gone, but the mill pond remains (attractively garnished with lilies these days), as does the hill down which the water

raced, known as 'Heart Attack Hill' among Camira employees who might (or might not) take a stroll up it at lunchtime.

Camira produce 9 million metres of fabric a year (not just moquette) in the UK and Lithuania. All the special Jacquard looms required for moquette are in Lithuania. According to Ciara Crossan, the Design Manager, 'Moquette will never go out of style, although fashions and trends change – there's certainly a growing movement, particularly in Europe, towards the contemporary look of vinyls and flat wovens (fabric without a pile). Moquette will always be a classic. It insulates against sound; it dyes beautifully; it has a power of flex and recovery; it's natural, so it's renewable and biodegradable.'

. . . Which brings us to the sheep. Whereas Holdsworth's favoured Colonial wool from the Southern Hemisphere, Camira use wool from cross-bred British sheep, mostly in the Scottish

Borders or around the Yorkshire Dales. These days, nylon is sometimes used to strengthen a moquette, to increase its resilience against the pressure of innumerable bottoms.

The publisher of this book and I spent the last half hour of our visit to Camira engaged in a sort of informal seminar on historical moquette with its encyclopaedically knowledgeable staff. On a long, high table, moquette samples and log books going back to the 1920s were laid out. All the Enid Marx and Marianne Dorn classics were there, as was Straub, and its variant for the national network, semi-officially titled 'Bournemouth', but more widely known among people younger than me as 'the Harry Potter moquette' because he sits on it in one of the films.

There was the beautiful Paris Metro moquette (see p. 137) with numerous rich colours (including light and dark green, maroon and purple), like the lining of a Paul Smith suit. I have often sat on that moquette, which is on the fast and driverless Line 14, known as the METEOR (Métro Est-Ouest Rapide).

There was a moquette from the Orient Express of the 1920s (a decadent floral in beige and blue) and another (see p. 10) from the *Flying Scotsman* train of the same decade: a depiction in dark blue and grey of overflowing classical fruit bowls. Somehow, I could extrapolate the whole train from those moquettes.

A corny phrase came to me about the Camira people: *dream weavers* . . .

GATE STOCK RATTAN

The trains called 'gate stock' had gates that were opened and closed by guards – or gatemen – standing on projections from the carriage ends. One guard stood between any two carriages. So a train of eight carriages needed six gatemen. The 'gate stock' trains – which were not the only stock to have gates – ran on the Yerkes Tubes, which is to say the lines that became the central part of the Bakerloo, Piccadilly and the West End Branch of the Northern Line. All these lines were built by the American financier, Charles Tyson Yerkes. Yerkes was a fraudster who had served time in the Eastern State Penitentiary in Philadelphia for shady dealings in the building of electric railways and tramways in the States. He came to London in 1899, when he was in his mid-sixties, accompanied by his mistress, 17-year old Emilie Grigsby, whose mother was the madam of a brothel in Cincinnati.

The aesthetic debt Londoners owe Yerkes is incalculable. His Tubes were – and mainly still are – very beautiful. They were designed by Leslie Green, Yerkes' young protégé architect, who died aged 33, it is said of overwork. Every station had a unique tiling scheme spelt out in tiles at the platform ends for the benefit of illiterate passengers who could not read the station names, and perhaps would also not catch the names shouted out by the outermost gatemen. (See the pale blues at Russell Square, or the creams, browns and mustards – chocolate sundae shades – at Regent's Park. When choosing a house or flat in central London, do try to live on a Yerkes Tube line.)

The gate stock carriages seem to have been commensurately charming. The last was withdrawn from the Piccadilly Line in 1923, and only a part of one survives – at the LT Museum's Acton depot. It is wood-panelled, like the billiard room of a country house. There were transverse seats in the centre, longitudinal ones at the ends. The seats on the exhibited vehicle are – and it is believed originally were – covered in an orangey rattan, an American style of seat covering, rather than moquette. At the time of writing, the New York Subway Museum is appealing for donations to help fund the restoration of some of its rattan seat coverings.

B-TYPE BUS

By 1909, the largest bus operator in London, the London General Omnibus Company, had so many types of buses that they'd almost reached the end of the alphabet in alphabetical classification. In that year, they manufactured the X-type, which was the breakthrough motor bus. They improved on it the following year, with the introduction of the B-type (the LGOC having by now started on a new alphabet). The B-type would become the

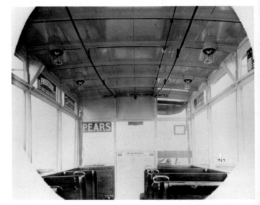

world's first mass-produced bus. It marked, according to Travis Elborough in *The Bus We Loved*, the start of the trail

that would lead to the Routemaster, the X-type being 'Cro-Magnon man to the Routemaster's *Homo sapiens*, if you will'.

The B-type eclipsed horse drawn buses, all of which were gone by 1915. But the B-type still had no roof; the upper deck was still called 'outside', and the 'outside' seats were wooden. On the lower deck was moquette, and a scrap of the one pictured was found in the LT Museum's B-type bus, when it was acquired in 2014. The

scrap showed a red and black pattern that seems floral if you focus on the black, geometric if you focus on the red. Holdsworth's of Halifax (see pp 120-1) generated a new moquette from the original sample, and the result is on the LT Museum's

B-type, and the one at the Museum's Acton depot. The LT Museum retails a sofa covered in this moquette. It is called

Pimlico, and its angular lines 'help promote a contemporary feel'.

EI TRAM

Electric trams came late to London – in 1901, by which time many provincial cities already had them. They were operated by London United Tramways in the western suburbs and used overhead wires. The London County Council, which controlled inner London, worried about the aesthetics of overhead wires, so its own trams, rolled out from 1903, collected their current from below.

Even the LCC trams never penetrated to the very centre of London, which partly accounts for the peculiar image of Edwardian trams: they were seen as highly modern but also downmarket. Trams had more capacity than buses, so the fares

could be cheaper, and trams catered to their working-class clients by starting earlier and finishing later. They bristled with 'No Spitting' signs, and carried adverts for populist phenomena such as the *News of the World*.

The LT Museum depot at Acton has a tram of the most common LCC type: an EI. Trams did not at this stage tend to have moquettes, and the seats downstairs on the EI are faux-leather, whilst those upstairs have the same stuff on the

cushion, but the backs are wooden. The upper decks were roofed over, trams being considered less likely to topple over than buses. But perhaps rooflessness would have been a virtue, because the top deck of trams (as with buses) saw smoking permitted, and there would be a higher percentage of smokers on a tram than a bus.

As the Twenties became the Thirties, the first generation of electric trams were beginning to look worn out and unfashionable compared to trolleybuses (which appeared in the capital from 1931). 'Pullmanisation' – a general smartening-up, including the introduction of moquette – was one answer. The black and white photograph shows one smart moquette, but the LT Museum depot has an LCC tram from the early 1930s that definitely seems to have been Pullmanised, judging by the orangey floral moquette on the lower deck.

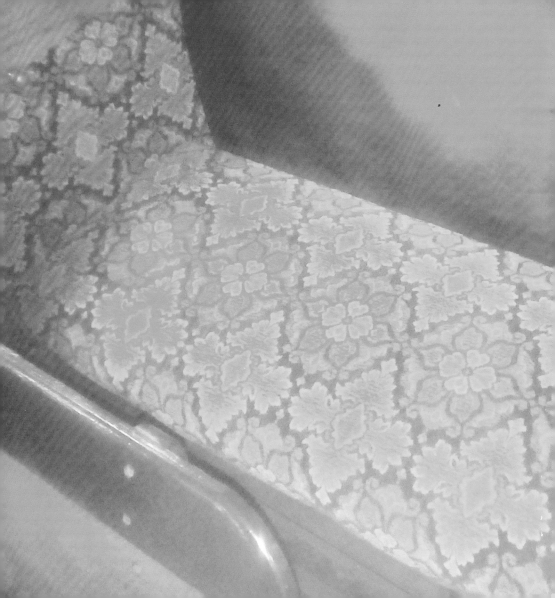

The impression we leave behind

A couple of years ago, as part of a university project on 'urban visual culture', Sarah Rathbone began taking pictures of the 'beautiful' (her word) London Underground moquettes.

Sarah is interested in the Tube. For another university project, she wrote an undergraduate dissertation on Underground visual culture and the way it has spread around the world (the roundel, for instance, is everywhere, copyright notwithstanding). Today, having left university, she is a junior graphic designer.

When I asked how her interest arose, she said, 'I was born in Greenwich, and now I live in Lewisham: I've travelled on the Tube all my life' — which is a very good reason, but then again many people who've travelled on the Tube all their lives have no interest in it whatsoever.

'Everyone sits on the seats,' says Sarah, 'but

they're under-appreciated, no-one notices them. They just sit down and look at their phones.' As though to rectify this moral imbalance, Sarah 'did not want the people' in her photographs, but she did want to show that the people had, so to speak, interacted with the seats unconsciously.

In every case, the seats she photographed had been vacated a moment before. Sometimes this is obvious, by virtue of a left-behind newspaper, or an indentation created by the buttocks of the departed. Sometimes there's a subtler indication: a pattern of light and shade where a spine pressed against the seat back. Sarah never manipulated the images, and sometimes there's hardly any indication of a recent occupation, but that some people departed the scene leaving no trace makes the images, to my mind, doubly poignant.

sarahrathbone.wixsite.com/rathbonedesign

LOZENGE

The forerunner of London Transport was the Underground Electric Railways Company of London, aka the Underground Group or 'the Combine'. It began as the organisation that ran the Underground lines of Charles Tyson Yerkes, but it acquired other networks, including, in 1913, the Central London Railway and the London General Omnibus Company. Its head of design, in effect (no such aesthetic titles existed at the time), was Frank Pick, who would eventually have the same role at London Transport.

As Publicity Officer, then Commercial Manager of the Underground Group, Frank Pick began the work for which he would become famous in the days of LT: this involved the harmonisation of transport iconography, so as to give the illusion that London was a coherent entity. For the Underground Group, Pick commissioned the roundel, the Johnston typeface and many posters by leading artists explaining or illuminating the system. We might think of this moquette – the first to be commissioned specially by the UERL, rather than purchased off the peg – as a modest element of this campaign. It became the company's standard moquette, and was used on Underground trains, trams, buses and trolleybuses.

I assume that Frank Pick was involved in its commissioning; its designer is unknown. The manufacturer (at least originally) was Firth Furnishings. In colour, it was an elegant and demure combination of teal and light brown, mainly the latter, which is an old railway colour. Peter Smith, author of *Station Colours*, says that the typical late-Victorian railway painter and decorator was equipped with a tin of white lead paint 'to which he added some pigment, sparingly, since the pigment was more expensive. Shades of brown were common; they were cheap and long lasting. Colours such as "stone" and "buff" were made by adding iron oxide to white lead and mixing with linseed oil . . .' He defines 'stone' as 'pale buff with a little yellow in the shade'. Buff itself is 'a darker shade that can approach brown'.

This moquette might be described as stone *or* buff. Being about the colour of dried mud, it wouldn't easily show the dirt. It also has a small repeat, so that it could be fitted to a variety of seats, and a tear be easily patched without disrupting the pattern.

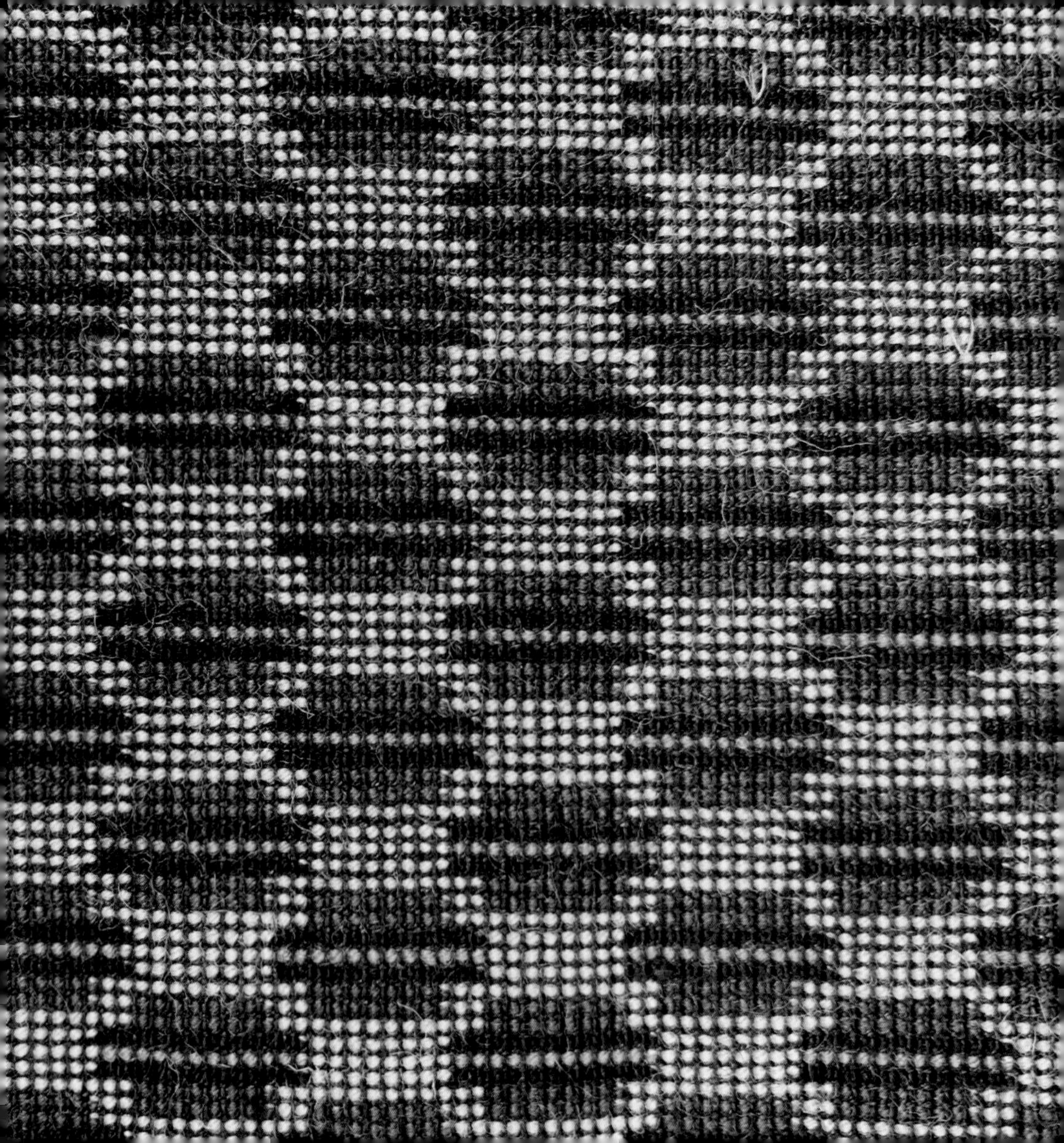

REVERSE-LOZENGE

Here is the Lozenge moquette of the previous page seen from the back. Moqeutte is usually backed with thin cotton, which is transparent, like tracing paper. I am told that curators at the London Transport Museum like to play 'Guess the moquette' – in other words seeing if they can identify a well-known moquette when viewed from the back. Sometimes a moquette viewed in this way seems much the same as when viewed from the front; others take on a whole new identity.

Another reason for revisiting the Lozenge moquette is that, as well as appearing on buses and trams, it was the first moquette on the Tube Standard Stock, which was introduced in 1923. The Standard Stock was the first to have air-controlled doors (no gates, in other words), but

otherwise there were a lot of variations *within* Standard Stock. Indeed, when I was writing a history of the Underground, one museum curator told me, 'The thing about Standard Stock is that it wasn't standard at all.' It included carriages of various lengths, for example, and they had various types of motors. The last Standard Stock trains were delivered in 1934, at which time they were on the Northern, Piccadilly and Bakerloo Lines.

In an article of 1989 for the *Journal of the Design History Society*, the fittingly named Cynthia Weaver wrote that this moquette 'marked a departure from the more domestic florals or the jazz-age fabrics which remained in service on London's transport throughout the 1930s.'

NS-TYPE BUS

Previous buses had sat on a chassis that was set above the wheels. For the NS-type, the Associated Equipment Company designed for the London General Omnibus Company a chassis that was stepped down between the axles. So the bus was low, requiring No Step, hence the name. But it might be (because the initials bestowed by AEC were often enigmatic) that NS stands for *Nulli Secundus*, or 'second to none'. I do hope so, but I suspect that theory comes from the type of people who call buses 'omnibuses'.

The low centre of gravity made the bus more stable than its predecessors; even so, the Metropolitan Police Carriage Office did not allow it to have a roof at first (so there would have been no moquette on the top-deck). But later versions did have a roof, and both types can be seen in the opening titles of *Piccadilly*, an excellent silent film of 1929 ('a sumptuous showbusiness melodrama seething with sexual and racial tension'). The titles begin with shots of Piccadilly Circus at night, with newly installed neon signs blazing forth louchely with 'Gordon's London Gin', 'Sandeman's Port' and 'Centre of the World'.

The buses then pull up in front of the camera, and, alongside their own decadent adverts ('Say Whisky and Schweppes'), there are posters giving the film's credits: 'British International Pictures Ltd . . . Piccadilly . . . an A. E. Dupont Production'. The atmosphere seems foggy, to which the passengers on the open-topped buses are contributing, since they're all smoking. This dark moquette of fawn, dark brown and red is believed to have been used on the early NS-types (along with Lozenge), and it too seems rather foggy.

It might be that the film's scriptwriter, Arnold Bennett, suggested this novel way of displaying the titles, since he was keen on buses, as we will be seeing.

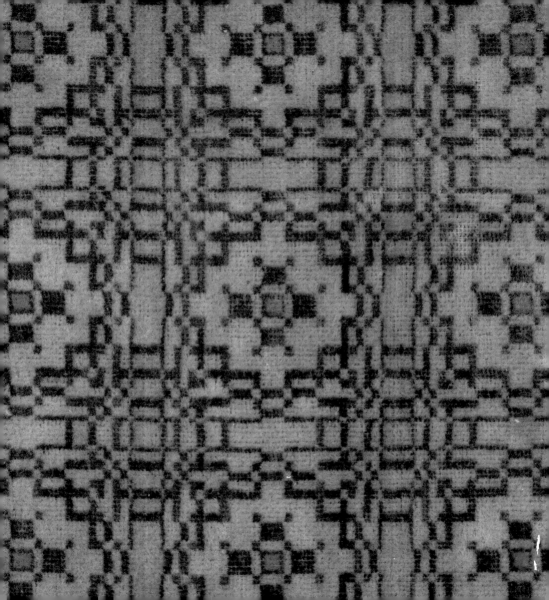

1st and 3rd Class

A class system obtained on the Metropolitan and District lines until 1941. By 1929 it was 1st and 3rd, and in these pictures showing compartments on the MW-Class trains (electric multiple units introduced on the Met in 1929) we have a glimpse of a moquette hierarchy. The price of your ticket might tell you which part of the train to sit in – but you could also find out by inspecting the moquette.

Even though we are on the brink of an era of intellectual, geometric moquettes, 1st-class types are still being rewarded with something exuberantly, luxuriantly floral or even jungly, whereas the lower orders must make do with a moquette that is more geometric, but only by virtue of sheer plainness rather than Modernist flair. (This moquette, incidentally, is similar to, and possibly the same as, the one used on the humble NS bus.)

Notice that the sign in this 1st-class compartment reads 'Smoking'. That's how it generally was in the first quarter of the 20th century, reflecting a disposition towards smoking. Where there was no 'Smoking' sign, you were not supposed to smoke, but 'No Smoking' signs were rare. They became more common after 1930, following a ruling by the superintendents of the Railway Clearing House, responding to the large number of complaints about passengers smoking in non-smokers. Third-class MW-Stock passengers *do* get 'No Smoking', as though emphasising the

severer regime.

The two moquettes opposite show the class system on the District Line Q Stock in 1935, with 1st class on the left, and 3rd class on the right. The Q stock had open carriages (no compartments), the classes separated, perhaps, by no more than a glass screen so you could see how the other half lived.

Both patterns, however, have their own opulence: the 1st class pattern is founded on a vibrant kingfisher blue, while 3rd class evokes classical statuary amidst rich golden tones.

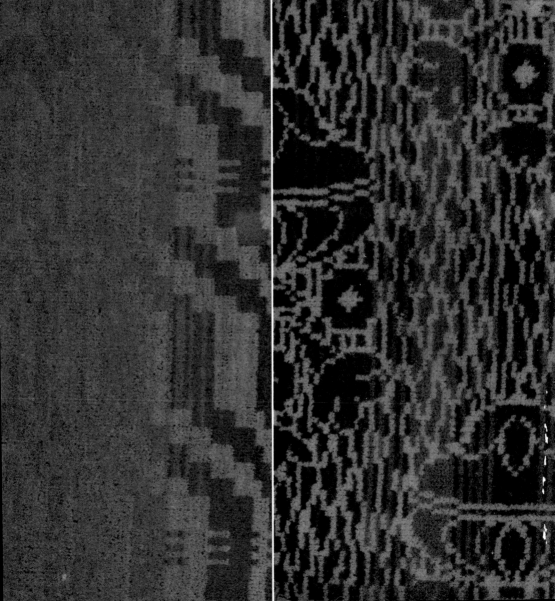

LT-TYPE BUS

Here, LT does not stand for London Transport, which will not exist for another four years. It denotes a double-decker six-wheeled bus called a Long T, which sounds like a ranch in Texas. The LT was one of a triumvirate of buses created from chasses built by AEC for the London General Omnibus Company in 1929, which by this time was a subsidiary of the Underground Group. The LT was 'Longer' than the T (right), a single decker, and the ST, or Short-type, was a double-decker with the standard four wheels. In all cases, advantage was taken of new maximum lengths permitted by the Metropolitan Police Public Carriage Office for London nuses.

The LTs (which had roofs) used petrol engines at first, but were later converted to diesel or 'oil', as it was called at the time. Early versions had open staircases. The bus had swagger and star

quality. 'Took one of the new 6-wheeled buses,' Arnold Bennett recorded in his *Journals* on 5 November 1928: 'just to try it, to the Ritz, and walked up to Bond Street to the Queen's Hall to look at programmes.' Given the date, he must be referring to a prototype.

(J. B. Priestley once wrote of Arnold Bennett's 'boyish enthusiasm for all that was metropolitan, fashionable, anything but provincial,' and attributed this to Bennett's being a 'super-provincial' himself.)

The bus persisted until the late 1940s, and it was the LT-type that Flanders and Swann evoked in their 1957 song 'A Transport of Delight', with its cumulative refrain about a big six-wheeler, scarlet-painted, London Transport, diesel engine, ninety-seven-horsepower omnibus.

The moquette associated with the LT (and ST and T) was this self-effacing, grey black and cream one. You might expect to see it on the kneelers in a mildewed country church. In the LT Museum (and now LT *does* stand for London Transport), there's a bulky, Forties-style three-piece suite covered in it.

LT-TYPE 1137

In the late 1920s, the London General Omnibus Company (which was owned by the Underground Group) began running Green Line bus services from countryside (which was increasingly suburbia) on one side of London to country places on the other side. The hub of the network was a bus station in Poland Street, Soho. (Talk about *rus in urbe*!)

In a brilliantly elemental marketing stroke, the buses were green, not red, and they had 'Green Line' written in gold on the sides. Both single and double-deckers were used. Some Green Line buses were ordinary red buses painted green; others were adapted – made more comfortable – for the long runs, and these were designated 'coaches'. In 1931, a Green Line-coach version of

the above-mentioned LT-type was created, and I use the definite article advisedly: only *one* was created, and it was for some mysterious reason given the number 1137. It was introduced on the service from Watford to Reigate (via London). Early on it had a sun roof (that is, a roof that slid open); it also had a clock and a rotary fan on the top deck. Even so, it was not popular with passengers. The door was at the front and the staircase was at the back, and, this being a long bus, it was a long walk from one to the other.

The moquette was almost riotously floral in an old-fashioned but charming way. We don't know the colour, having only this black and white photograph, but my bet is that green was involved.

No. 1137 was retired from active service during the War and scrapped in 1946.

FELTHAM TRAM

The Feltham tram, developed by a private operator and London United Tramways, a subsidiary of the Underground Group, was another answer to the growing image of trams as lumbering and antiquated compared to trolleybuses. The Feltham was built in the suburb of Feltham by the Union Construction Company, who had built the Underground Standard Stock and would build the 'Diddler' trolleybus (see p. 44).

The Felthams came ready-Pullmanised. They were that paradoxical thing: an elite tram. They usually had leather seats on the upper and lower

decks; sliding air-closed doors, and the driver had an actual cab and a seat, as opposed to the traditional arrangement, where he would stand on an open platform, like the helmsman of a boat. They were also the fastest trams in Europe, but they came too late save the tram in London. A Royal Commission of 1931 recommended motor buses and trolleybuses as the way forward, and this would be the direction of travel of London Transport Passenger Board, when it was formed in 1933.

I have said that the Felthams 'usually' had leather seats, but this brown and gold moquette has an intriguing wavelike effect that hints at

Morse code recorded on ancient parchment, was apparently used on both trams and trolleybuses during the Thirties. The Feltham at the National Tramway Museum at Crich in Derbyshire, on the other hand, has this attractively low-key grey-ish moquette. The moquette is newly fitted but is a re-creation of the moquette believed to have been used on the tram when new.

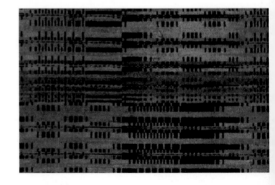

STL-TYPE BUS

This moquette was associated with the STL bus, which was introduced in 1934. It was the first mass-produced diesel bus, and would become *the* London bus of the 1930s and 1940s. The STL was a development of the ST (Short Type) and the above-mentioned LT (Long Type), and STL might stand for 'Short Type Longer', a name so unimaginative as to be almost imaginative. In his book about the Routemaster, *The Bus We Loved*, Travis Elborough wrote of the STL:

> It had a large, sit-up-and-beg front radiator, an enclosed staircase, a rear platform with a pole, and an upper deck that extended over the top of the driver's cab, allowing more seats upstairs. In the genealogy of London buses, you'd probably finger it as the Routemaster's great uncle, the suave elderly bachelor with the fondness for vintage wines and a cheroot perennially on the go.

That enclosed staircase had a mirror at the top, which was eventually removed because, according

to (sexist) legend, too many women stopped to look at themselves in it. There were many types of STLs, including – for the 108

route – the 'Tunnel STLs' that could fit through the Blackwall Tunnel, thanks to a tapered roof profile, and these had one fewer seat on the upper deck – a somehow haunting fact. According to the excellent website, *Ian's Bus Stop*, anyone yawning widely in South blah London in the days of the STLs was likely to provoke the comment, 'Look out, here comes an STL.' The Tunnel STLs kept running through the Blackwall Tunnel until 1953, when it was widened.

There were both Green Line and Country Area STLs and this blue-green moquette (the one most commonly associated with the STLs, seen here on RT1) would have harmonised nicely with their green exteriors and the passing landscape. It is a green of light and dark shades, like a shadowy forest, and the thin beige stripe looks golden in the right light.

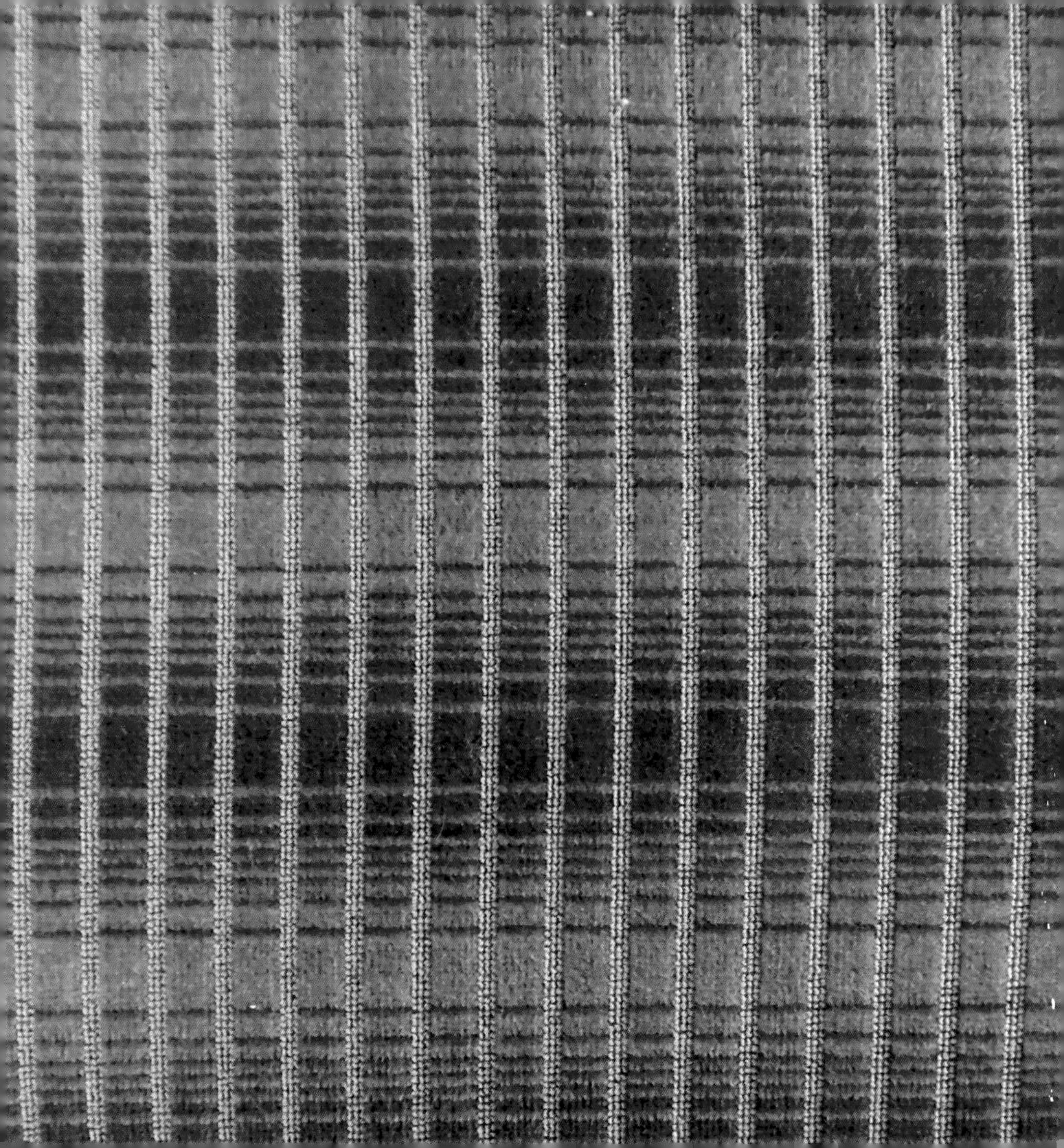

DIDDLER TROLLEYBUS

A trolleybus is a cross between a bus and a tram. Trolleybuses, like trams, were dependent upon an overhead power line, but they were more manoeuvrable than trams, not being on rails. This apparent freedom, however, only reflected their demeaning role, which was to get out of the way of cars. Trolleybuses lived their short London life between 1931 and 1962, during which time London accumulated the largest fleet in the world, so there were many varieties. But even a fansite for them (and there aren't many of those) admits, 'A trolleybus is a trolleybus is a trolleybus.'

One type – officially the A1s, being the first ones in London – was characterful enough to earn a nickname: the Diddler, so called because, compared to a tram, it could 'diddle about' in the road. It was the only trolleybus with a half cab, so it was not as slab-like as the others. From today's perspective,

it looks like a Routemaster with antennae. Like all trolleybuses it has six wheels, and the Diddler was modelled on the six-wheeler LT bus, introduced the previous year. (See pp. 36, 38)

The Diddler preserved at the London Bus Museum has this lovely leaf pattern, like autumnal leaves fallen into a wintry pond. Moquettes were beginning to be geometrical, but this one is a throwback to the floral moquettes that predominated on pre-grouping railways, which seemed designed simply to be as pretty as possible. 'For the decoration of carriage interiors', wrote Brian Haresnape of that unsystematic era in his book *British Rail 1948-83, A Journey by Design*, 'it was often the wife of the General Manager or of one of his senior staff who chose furnishings and fabrics . . .'

1938 and all that

By the 1930s, Frank Pick (below) was the biggest fish in the small pond of British industrial design. Given the haphazard development of that discipline in Britain, it seems about right that Pick had no artistic training but was merely an aesthetic man who, as second-in-command of the Underground Group, applied the principle of elegant utility (watchword of the Design Industries Association, of which he was a member) to mass transit.

In the mid-1930s Pick, now CEO at London

Transport, gave moquette his full attention. The trigger was the New Works Programme of 1935, a £40 million investment that would fund line extensions and a new generation of Tube trains, in particular the 1938 Tube Stock, which were technologically advanced but also had the cosiest transport interiors until the Routemaster came along.

Pick entrusted the job of commissioning moquette designs for these and other trains to his publicity officer, a former architect called Christian Barman. Barman first approached the prolific

Swiss-born textile designer, Marianne Straub, but she wasn't happy with the brief, and would not supply a moquette to LT until the 1960s.

Enid Marx (left and right), on the other hand, found Barman's brief 'perfect', and she produced at least four moquettes for him. (On page 48 is her sketch for the later design that would become Chevron.) Marx had been born in London in 1903, a second cousin twice removed of Karl Marx ('He's supposed to be a relative, but I think he's bogus.') She was expensively schooled at Roedean, where an eccentric headmistress encouraged her in botanical drawing and carpentry. In her artistic training – at the Central School of Arts and Crafts and the RCA – Marx was taught by the Modernist painter Paul Nash, who would also supply two moquette designs to Christian Barman (neither was ever applied to a train). Marx had found Nash inspiring, but she found another of her eminent tutors, Edward Johnston (from whom Pick had commissioned the Underground's radical, sans serif typeface) tedious. Prior to working for LT, Marx had mainly produced block prints on textiles and paper.

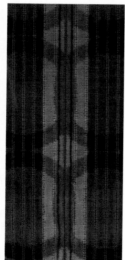

Marion Dorn also supplied about four moquettes. Dorn was American; she'd moved to London in 1923, and began producing scarves, curtains and carpets for prestigious clients including Claridge's, the Savoy Hotel and Cunard for its ocean liners. She was married to Edward McKnight Kauffer, the most radical of the poster designers commissioned by Pick, who produced stunningly modernist designs like 'Power' opposite – a true power couple of the Underground. 'She could see things through precise mental images of texture, colour and form,' wrote her obituarist in the *Guardian* in 1994. 'The gift stemmed from childhood years immobilised by TB, when she developed visual recall long before she could write.'

In *Underground Movement*, Paul Moss summarises the overall brief given by Barman: 'The fabrics had to be pleasing in both natural and artificial light and not create "dazzle" when in motion. It was suggested that the new patterns should be seen as a symbol of the Underground's unification of the country and city.'

Accordingly, the principal colours involved would be red and green, symbolic of the distinction between town and country, which Frank Pick was keen to stress. In 1926, in a paper for the Institute of Transport, he had lamented the way that London was 'sprawling out amoeba-like, surrounding and absorbing the villages that lie on its borders.' It was the Underground, of course, that was largely responsible for this, particularly the Northern Line in its northern reaches and the Metropolitan Line with its shameless development of Middlesex into the new suburbs of Metroland, and Pick would die, in 1941, a disappointed man and a strong supporter of the Green Belt.

But throughout his career, Frank Pick had showered Londoners with aesthetic gifts, and the moquettes he commissioned (via Barman) are an important – if overlooked – part of his legacy.

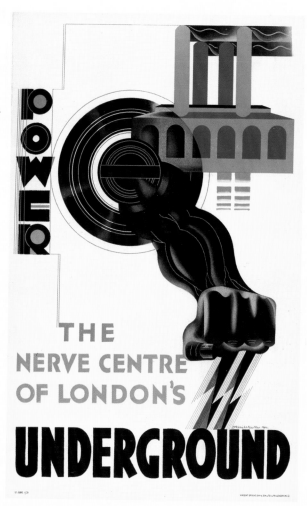

THE NERVE CENTRE OF LONDON'S UNDERGROUND

COLINDALE or LEAF

We now come to the series of moquettes commissioned by Christian Barman, London Transport Publicity Officer, on behalf of Frank Pick, head of design (in effect) at LT. These moquettes, considered classics of the genre, were first used on the 1938-Stock trains, and for the background to this enterprise see '1938 And All That', on p. 46.

On the Standard Stock trains that preceded the 1938-Stock, you might have been sharing your carriage – if you were sitting in a driving car – with one of the motors distributed along the length of the train. On the 1938s, all the motors were below the carriage floors, so you didn't have to concern yourself over the whereabouts of such unpleasant-sounding things as driving bogies. On these new trains, the passenger came first. In *London's*

Underground, John Glover wrote of the 1938s that they were 'probably the most comfortable trains that have ever run on the Underground'. They were fitted with deep, well-sprung seats, and the *Railway Engineer* magazine of October 1937 noted the 'cheerful colouring' of the interiors, which were mainly green and cream.

Enid Marx had been told by Christian Barman, who commissioned the moquettes, that green was regarded as lending a 'serene atmosphere'; that it promoted 'the feeling of being in the country when you were really in a tunnel'; also that 'it doesn't change as much as some colours do when going from one type of lighting to another.' The green would frequently be paired with red, partly for the effective colour contrast, partly to symbolise town and country.

The 1938 trains would go onto the Bakerloo, Northern, Central, Piccadilly and East London Lines, and perhaps the major contributor of moquettes to the 1938s was Marion Dorn. We know that her red and green leaves-on-the-vine design – much more readily explained by one of its names ('Leaf') than by the alternative title ('Colindale') – went on to the 1938s, first appearing (probably) on the Northern and Bakerloo Lines. Its pattern embodies the transition between the old order of floral designs and the new of geometric repetition.

BELSIZE or GRID

Enid Marx's first moquettes were intended for the interiors of the flat-fronted prototypes of the 1938 stock, but would later be used elsewhere. She was permitted to use larger pattern repeats than those traditionally used by LT, in the hope of avoiding the flicker or 'dazzle' associated with a fussy pattern moving at speed. And she recalled that her moquettes were required 'to look fresh at all times, even after bricklayers have sat on it.'

Grid, as its name suggests, is rectilinear and geometric: in *Enid Marx, The Pleasures of Patterns*, Alan Powers describes it as 'something between a Frank Lloyd Wright window and an out-of-step tartan'. In the block-printed textiles with which she had made her name, however, Marx had favoured natural forms (see p. 46). 'One associates floral motifs with the home rather than with public transport,' she said in an interview of 1986 with Cynthia Weaver. 'I don't think any of us would have thought of using floral motifs for buses, or trains, or aeroplanes.' When told

that many early moquettes *were* florals, she said, 'Well, I'm blowed.'

We will be seeing further Marx moquettes. I once visited an art bookshop in York, whose proprietor had the feistiness that was apparently a characteristic of Marx herself. I naïvely asked this woman whether she had ever heard of Enid Marx. '*Of course* I've heard of Enid Marx,' she said. 'I'm often in London, and I think of her every time I go on the Tube.'

CANONBURY or HANDCUFF and CALEDONIAN

Another of Marion Dorn's designs to feature on the 1938s was known as 'Canonbury' or 'Handcuff'. It involved wide green and beige stripes overlaid with a brown chainlink pattern. Dorn also produced a bold check called Caledonian for the 1938s.

A theme is emerging: Colindale, Canonbury, Caledonian; later on Dorn would produce a moquette called Chesham. It seemed that a kind of alphabetical game was played in the nomenclature of these 1930s classic moquettes.

In the mid-Thirties Imperial Airways had set the tone for this kind of alliteration with its fleet of airliners, and most famously its glamorous 'C-Class' flying boats plying the Empire Airmail

routes – individually christened *Canopus*, *Ceres*, *Corsair*, *Corinthian* and others.

Most of Dorn's patterns, therefore, would be labelled with the name of a Tube station beginning with C. Caledonian must allude to Caledonian Road on the Piccadilly Line, and has an appropriately tartan effect; Canonbury stretches the point slightly by presumably referring to what was then a British Railways station (and is now on the Overground).

Enid Marx's Tube station names would start with B; Paul Nash's with A. It is likely that all the 'C' moquettes of Marion Dorn strayed beyond the 1938-Stock Tube trains, appearing on sub-surface trains as well . . .

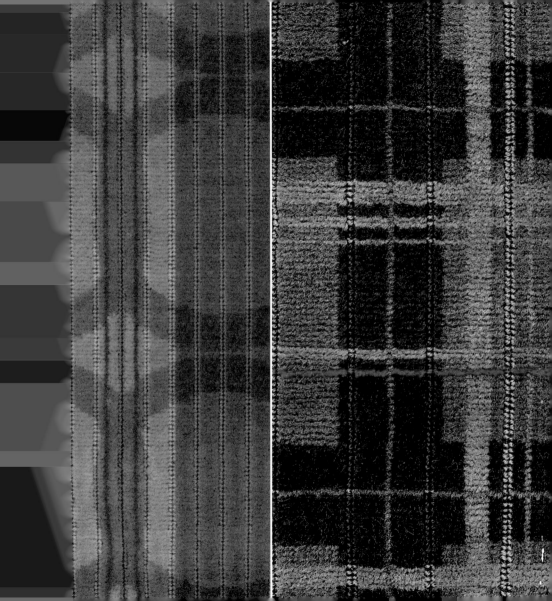

BUSHEY

Bushey was another early moquette Enid Marx designed for Christian Barman, and was a more conventional tartan. But with these designs she found a frustrating dislocation between what she submitted and the finished fabric, especially after the painstaking thread-by-thread plotting displayed in this handwritten diagram.

> *I was given the specification of 12.5" [inches] or multiples thereof, into which the design must repeat, and I adhered to this in all the sketches I submitted. When the woven samples arrived, it was apparent . . . that they were very different from the original drawing . . . The pattern had been altered, presumably to suit technical requirements, without regard to proportion or weight, and had lost all character.*

According to Alan Powers, in *Enid Marx: The Pleasures of Pattern*, the irascible Marx would take away from her 'Underground experience' 'a frustration that became almost a fixation about manufacturers' unwillingness to take her seriously as a collaborator in the technical processes, rather than just a producer of drawings'.

These early patterns, blending rather earthy tones of brown, beige and ochre, were a learning experience for Marx in another respect.

> *We all thought at first that the best way of disguising dirt was to use colours which would more or less tone in with the dirt, but we subsequently discovered that this was a false assumption, and that the best method of ensuring the seats would look clean after a period of use was to use strongly contrasting tones and rather brilliant colour: they remained more vigorous than a design which was in the first place rather subtle in tone. This subtlety turned to drabness.*

We will see the difference with Marx's later moquettes.

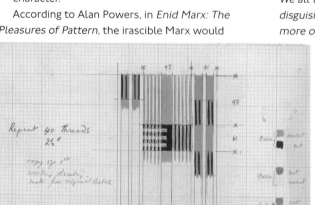

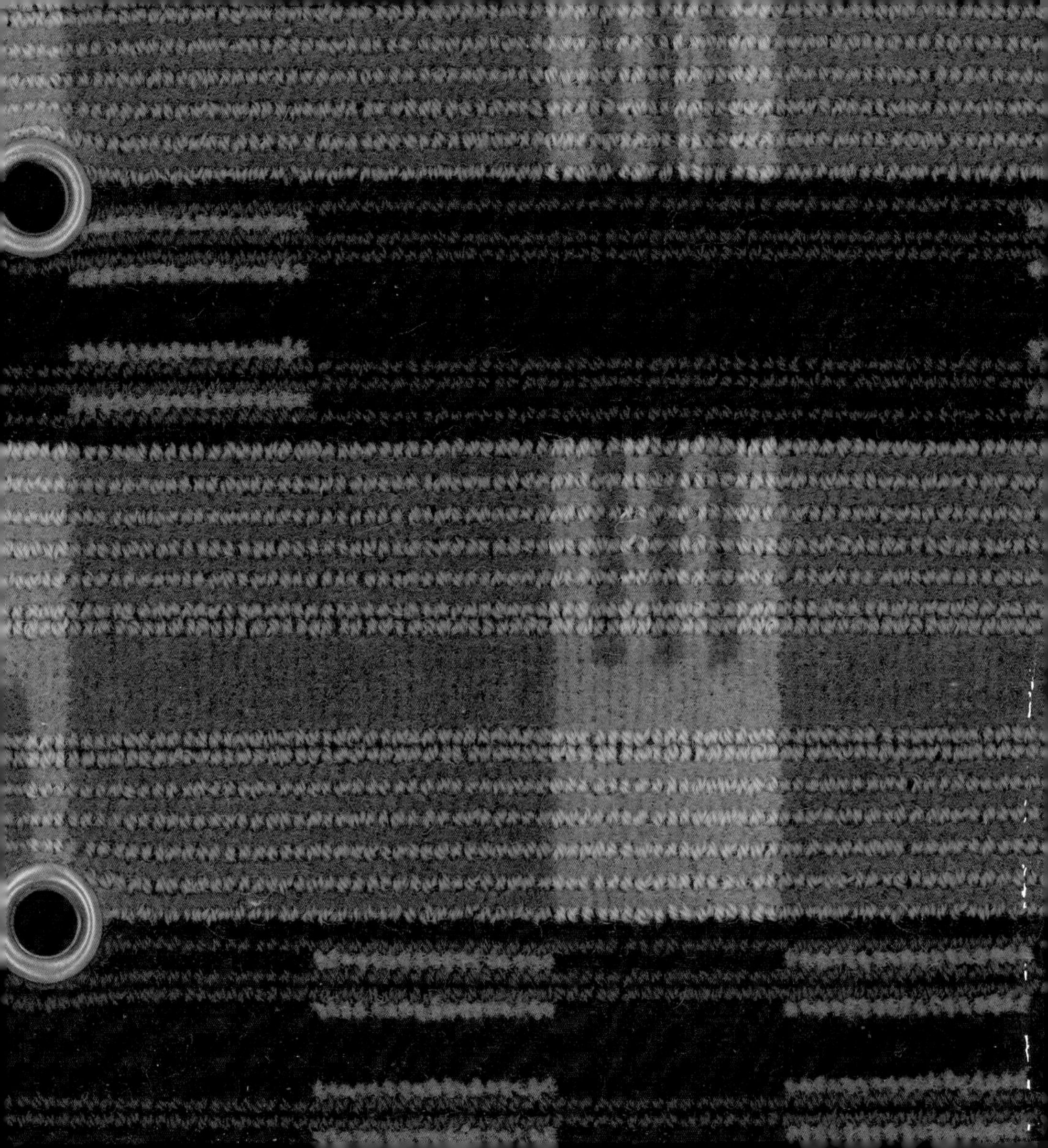

CHESHAM or LADDER and BRENT or DOUBLE DIAMOND 🪑🪑🪑🪑🪑

I will mention these two classics with reference to the O-Stock trains, which were for the sub-surface lines and which, like the 1938-Stock, appeared in 1938. Like the 1938-Stocks they were comfortable, externally red, and built under the enlightened engineering regime of Graff-Baker. The Os went initially onto the Hammersmith &

City section of the Metropolitan (the H&C not yet being a line its own right). Like the experimental 1935 Stock, they had flared sides, giving them a bell-like profile, and there was no running board under the doors, in case people – encouraged by the flared shape – should try to leap aboard a moving train.

This linear design of Marion Dorn's called 'Chesham' or 'Ladder' went onto the O-Stock, as did Enid Marx's red diamonds on a green grid, called 'Brent'. Judging from period black-and-white photographs 'Ladder' originally had a paleish blue colourway, but it seems to have been re-coloured around 1950 in red.

PAUL NASH

It is logical that the multi-talented Paul Nash should have been invited by Christian Barman to contribute to the 1938-stock moquettes. In 1921, some of Nash's textile designs had been exhibited at the most aesthetic of department stores, Heal's, and in 1936, he designed posters for LT encouraging the use of season tickets. (They resembled pages from a radical scrapbook, combining photographs and both figurative and semi-abstract illustration.)

Nash was becoming increasingly interested in applied arts, and in 1930 he became a founder member of the Society of Industrial Artists. All that said, his moquette designs are a footnote in his career (and not even that in his autobiography, *Outline*). This might be explained by the fact that Nash suffered badly from asthma in the mid-1930s.

The fate of Nash's designs remains obscure. In *Enid Marx, The Pleasures of Pattern* Alan Powers records that Alperton (on the right) was the very first moquette pattern to be commissioned by London Underground, as early as 1928, and originally intended for the seating at the showpiece new Piccadilly Circus station.

But Powers also quotes Marx herself as telling Nikolaus Pevsner that neither of Nash's designs ever went into production (at least, we can assume, on a train).

A sample of Alperton does survive, and very elegant it is, albeit somewhat faded. The muted colour palette is reminiscent of the paintings Nash had produced as an official War Artist on the Western Front, some of which were based on sketches he called 'fifty drawings of muddy places.' Those muddy places are subsumed, you feel, in this abstract moquette.

The second moquette, Arnos, or at least the black-and-white photograph of it below, in an unidentified magazine, which is all we have, resembles, fittingly enough, an un-filled-in crossword puzzle. We don't know the colour of

this moquette, though the magazine's caption writer sums up the various 1938 moquettes pictured along with Arnos as being 'sensible colourings – browns and soft greens chiefly – and of a character of which passengers will not tire too quickly.'

Art Deco, Streamline Moderne, the Jazz Age and...moquette

The interwar era was the great age of art deco in design and fashion, and when Frank Pick became Chief Executive of London Transport in the Twenties, with the intention of unifying the design brief across the organisation, it led to some of the landmarks of the style across the capital.

There was Charles Holden's architecture, creating LT's headquarters at 55 Broadway, and the stations along the Piccadilly Line. Piccadilly Circus Station in particular, with its opulent, smooth, polished surfaces and extravagant curves, heralds the later manifestation of art deco in the Thirties, Streamline Moderne. This was the age of the ocean liners, and of the machine age, and, where the earlier art deco of the Jazz Age had drawn on influences as disparate as ancient Egypt and China for its

more angular geometry of zigzags and chevrons, now there was a preoccupation with evoking the speed and kinetic power of the city.

Streamline Moderne can be seen in the prototype Tube train that preceded the 1938 Stock,

and in the Q-type buses of the time, especially the double-deck version, and there's an evident kinship with the arrestingly avant garde posters by 'Andrew Power', the pseudonym of the partnership of the linocut artists Sybil Andrews and Cyril Power.

So what about the moquette of the time? Marion Dorn, one of the first wave of designers commissioned by Christian Barman, designed fabrics for some of the great art deco projects in London: the Savoy Hotel, Claridges and Eltham Palace, like this rug still adorning its sensational entrance hall. But you'd struggle to see a moquette like Colindale (see p. 50-1) as art deco – it's rigidly geometric and something of a throwback to the earlier era of floral patterns.

Perhaps the answer's to be found in this Cyril Power linocut of a Tube train interior from 1934. It's all swaying movement and speed, an almost claustrophobic evocation of the sensory overload of crowded Tube travel. But there, in the background, is the first depiction of a moquette pattern on the Tube – and it's squarely repetitive, geometric . . . and in its small way rather comforting.

Enid Marx explains her fellow designers' brief: 'Joggling and the frequent use of artificial light were liable to produce dazzle, and the designs must reduce this rather than accentuate.' In other words, there was quite enough movement and kinesis coming at Tube passengers already without the moquette adding to it. These early

repeating squares, verging on tartans, were pacifying, even restful. Significantly, the Jazz Age busyness of this moquette on the streamlined prototype Tube train was not used on the production stock.

But look at this moquette used on the STL buses during the Thirties – pure art deco. In general it seems to have been the buses that saw the more jazzy, extravagant moquettes (consider the interior of this Q-type country bus), and perhaps the reason is that a ride on a lumbering bus would have been less of a sensory overload, and its interior was most of the time lit with natural light. The harlequin moquette below was used on the District Line in 1933: a sub-surface line whose wide carriages had high ceilings and spent most of their journeys above ground.

Strangely, Enid Marx seems later to have embraced art deco with enthusiasm, with the sweeping curves of Shield and, harking back to its earlier era, indeed, the bold Chevron or Zigzag (see pp. 74-75).

WAR: MOQUETTE-FREE AUSTERITY

When the Blitz began in September 1940, many buses were put out of action, perhaps most famously the double decker blown against the side of a house in Mornington Crescent on 9 September 1940. Eleven people died; they had been in the houses rather than on the bus, whose passengers and crew had been sheltering. The advert on the side of the bus seems to signify a lost progressivism: 'Hovis: Not *Just* Bread'.

Later in the War, buses would become 'just buses' . . .

With private motoring all but banned, there was a high demand for bus journeys, but production had ceased, the usual manufacturers producing tanks and lorries. In mid-1941 the Ministry of Supply permitted the building of basic 'utility' or austerity buses, which would be built by Guy, Daimler and Bristol. 'The first batch had sprung leather seats,' wrote Oliver Green in *Bus Fare*, 'but most later austerity vehicles entered service with wooden slatted seating.' Londoners suddenly found themselves travelling back in time to the days of the 'garden seats' of the 1880s

Sometimes, as with the Guy bus at the London Bus Museum, the leather was not leather but faux-leather, and where the seats were wooden, the wood was unseasoned, so that a schoolboy in shorts (say) might end up with a splinter in his bum.

And as if to confirm that red had been a rather exuberant and indulgent colour for buses, the austerity buses were often not red, but a more muted and unobtrusive red oxide (in other words, brown). With dipped headlights, no rear windows and dim interiors (and anti-blast netting at the window) these buses groped their way through the blackout, the first sign of their approach to a bus stop being a flash of the white paint that had been daubed on their mudguards (left), which was in fact a slightly dandyish feature, as if they were wearing spats.

RT

The RT (Regent Type) bus, introduced in 1939, took the baton passed by the STL: it became the standard London double-decker of the 1950s, and was more widespread in the capital than any other bus. It is often paid the backhanded compliment of being seen as the precursor of the Routemaster. But some people hold the apparently heretical position that the RT was better than the Routemaster. One was the architectural historian, Gavin Stamp. 'There was something slightly stodgy about its unfashionable and ungimmicky appearance,' wrote Stamp of the Routemaster in his book *Anti-Ugly*.

> *No, the most elegant public conveyance ever to grace the streets of London was its predecessor, the RT . . . Slightly narrower than the Routemaster while having the same rounded corners and interior treatment, it was characterised by a more pronounced slope at*

the front, curving back from its vertical radiator, while the rear was proudly vertical end display.

Whereas the RMs had their own moquette right from the start, the moquette most closely associated with the RT was not applied until the late 1940s. It featured black, pale green and brown horizontal stripes in cut pile (to give a velvety feel), with thin, red vertical stripes in loop or uncut pile (giving a rougher feel). It was also used on RF and GS-type single-deckers, and on some late trolleybuses.

Did its use on a great many green London Country buses determine this moquette's earthy tones? The publisher of this book's memories of grinding to school on RTs on red route 54 and green 403 are of their interiors feeling exceedingly frowsy by the Seventies, particularly on the smoke-clogged top deck.

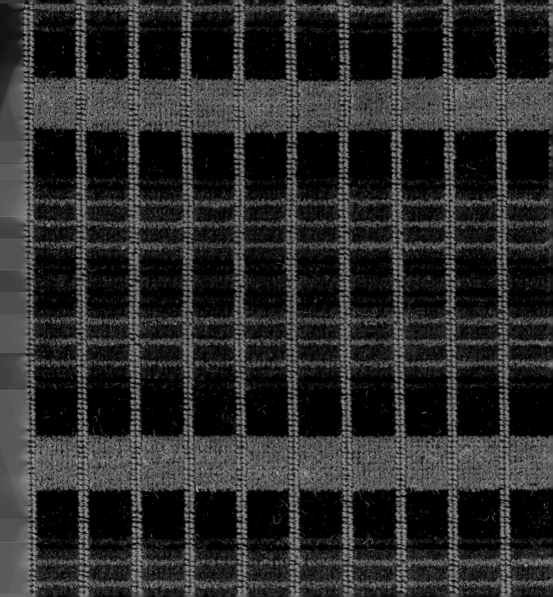

QI CLASS TROLLEYBUS

Unlike buses, trams and trolleybuses did not undergo a period of decadence. They just kept getting better until they were abolished. The QIs were the only post-war trolleybuses; they were also the last, and known as 'the Rolls Royce of trolleybuses'. At the time of writing, the London Bus Museum has QI number 1812 (on loan from the Trolleybus Museum at Sandcroft), which operated the last trolleybus service to run from Uxbridge to Hanwell Broadway on 8 November 1960. It has this wild, abstract moquette in pink and at least two shades of green. The QI trolleybus at the LT Museum depot in Acton has the same moquette.

The trolleybuses had been introduced to be more manoeuvrable than trams, but they were not manoeuvrable enough, and would outlast trams by only ten years, being withdrawn in

1962 to make way for the new Routemaster bus. The Routemaster was much loved, but it edged out vehicles that were both quieter and more environmentally friendly.

London had the largest trolleybus fleet in the world, but it's as if they never existed. I discovered that there had been one of those nest-like arrangements of overhead wires that formed a trolleybus turning-circle bang in the middle of Highgate, where I have lived for 20 years. Today it is where the buses turn around. Nobody in what we like to call 'the village' had ever mentioned this to me.

Incidentally, 125 of the 127 QI trolleybuses retired (like many of the people who rode in them) to Spain.

SHIELD and CHEVRON

After the war, the commissioners of the 'classic' moquettes, Frank Pick and Christian Barman, were no longer at LT. Pick had died in 1941; Barman worked in publicity for the Transport Commission until his retirement – with an OBE for services to transport – in 1963. (He died in 1980.) Nonetheless, a number of moquettes commissioned by them before the War, or commissioned in spirit of that enlightened partnership, were introduced, mainly for the refurbishment of the 1938-Stock trains.

Two of the best-known and best-liked of Enid Marx's moquettes were used in this way. All featured the symbolically important red-green dyad, and with both Marx had very definitely learned her lesson from Belsize and Bushey and eschewed paler, 'dirty' shades in favour of rich, glowing tones.

One was Shield, which seems to have had no subtitle derived from a Tube station name and which had a flowing motif involving repetition of what looked like the Christian ichthys. It appears

briefly on a British Transport Films newsreel of 1956 called *Looking at Transport*, the theme of which is the aesthetic success of London Transport. As usual, moquette gets short shrift. Shield appears in a montage with bus stops and litter bins, all of which, according to the voiceover, 'achieve a decorative effect'.

At about the same time, and for the same purpose (1938-Stock refurb), she also produced the very purposeful-looking 'Chevron' which, again, seems to have no Tube station subtitle.

ROUNDEL or BULLSEYE

Another design used on the 1938 Stock refurbishments was an attractive, if fairly literal, representation of the Underground roundel, known as Roundel or Bullseye. It had long been attributed to Eddie Chapman, head designer at the moquette manufacturers Holdsworth's. But the moquette researches of London Transport Museum curator Georgia Morley uncovered a letter of 1947 from a manager at Holdsworth's to London Transport: 'We have the pleasure in enclosing a new trial of the design made by Miss Jarvis, with the horizontal bar of the "Underground" symbol strengthened...' Another letter, of 1948, refers to the same moquette: 'Design number 11521 . . . this has been used recently in 1938 Tube stock . . . this is a Joy Jarvis pattern. Miss Jarvis is a very young and new designer recommended to me.'

GREEN LINE

When London Transport inherited the Green Line network, it was incorporated into a so-called Country Area of green buses and coaches. Country Area buses operated mostly radially, from London suburbs like Croydon and Enfield out into the Home Counties, and Green Line coaches crossed the full diameter of London on lengthy routes from one far-flung outpost like Westerham to another on the other side like Aylesbury. Both London Country and Green Line services penetrated deep into Hertfordshire, Essex, Kent, Surrey and Berkshire.

The Country Area buses never had a special moquette, but after the War the Green Line coaches were supplied with one, and it

perpetuated the green/red fixation discussed earlier, being olive green, dark green and red. 'As every student of art knows,' writes James Hulme in 'Green Line and Country Area Services' in *Bus Fare: Collected Writings on London's Most Loved Means of Transport*, 'red and green are oppositional, complementary colours – the dramatic optical effect wherever town and country networks met was quite sensational.' The green

and red symbolised the romantic, and increasingly untenable idea (given the growth of the suburbs) that the town was the town and the country was the country.

This moquette was introduced in 1952, on the typical Green Line coach of the time, the single-decker RF (standing for Regent Four). This had the flowing, slightly melted look of the Routemaster that would appear a decade later. Both buses were designed by Douglas Scott. In his book on Scott, Jonathan Glancey wrote of the RF that it 'appeared to have been extruded from one long piece of curved sheet steel. It was a streamlined vehicle almost completely free of appendages. The windows, a more or less continuous band of glazing, were set flush in the bodywork.' And the greenery would have sped by, echoing that of the moquette which, according to Glancey, was designed by R. Ingles and N. Dutton.

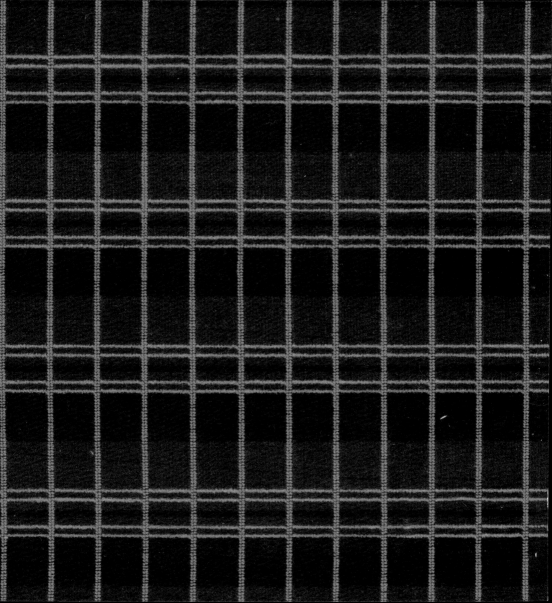

Cat's Guide to Moquette

Cats do not take the Tube, at least under their own steam. (Pigeons are another matter, especially on the Hammersmith & City Line, especially in the Ravenscourt Park area.) But they do have strong opinions on moquette patterns (as on most things), as the London Transport Museum's Assistant Director of Collections and Engagement Chris Nix can testify to his cost.

Chris has quite a lot of moquette furniture, which his four Norwegian forest cats, he admits ominously, 'love, and see as theirs'.

It didn't take long for me to spot they had preferences, and then to realise the logical reason for their preference. They most like moquettes such as D78 and Routemaster – clawing and rubbing their heads on it. With Colindale/ Leaf they like sitting on it but not clawing it. Once they'd damaged enough material for me to spot this I realised that they prefer the moquettes that are a mix of cut and loop (D78 & Routemaster), as they can catch their claws on the loops to sharpen them and scent mark (whilst wrecking the loops). I quickly switched to buying cut moquette (Colindale), which they still like but don't destroy.

Here is Toksvig the ginger cat forced to merely prowl around on Shield moquette, and Mags the grey contemplating the challenge of a temporarily pristine Routemaster stool. The Green Line ottoman is an example of their best work they prepared earlier.

This kind of vandalism would normally be a matter for the British Transport Police, but fortunately for Toksvig and Mags they are cats.

TROLLEYBUS AND LAST TRAM

This strikingly mournful moquette, reminiscent of a jigsaw with pieces missing, was used on trolleybuses from the mid-1930s. One curator told me it had also been used on trams in their final years. He was absolutely certain of this, but had forgotten *why* he was certain.

The last night of the London trams was 5 July 1952. Trams were 'the people's' mode, and all that day crowds lined the streets as the trams (to quote the London Transport press office) 'said goodbye to London'. It was an emotional occasion, not least because the trams would be incinerated immediately afterwards.

A beautiful newsreel film, *The Elephant Will Never Forget*, was made about that day, the title a reference to the south London hub and famous pub sign. The film is on You Tube and I defy anyone (even if they've never *heard* of London trams) not to be moved by it. It is in part

a celebration, to the raucous strains of a music hall singalong, 'The Tram Car Song', about romance on the top deck of a tram car. Some interiors are glimpsed: the seats are usually leather, or faux-leather. One moquette is disclosed, between the knees of a schoolboy collecting tram numbers, but it is floral, not this one.

The film then goes into a minor key: solo violin and shots of trams in nocturnal rain: 'We'll remember the rattle and the clang and the sway,' runs the commentary, 'and how snug it was to be inside when it was raining outside. It's a funny thing really, but the trams and the rain and the streets of South London all seemed to belong together.'

The moody colours of this moquette (they'd never be sanctioned today) suggest the London sky on a rainy night. Every time I see it I think of that film, and Lord Latham, Chairman of London Transport, giving his speech when the last tram had rolled into New Cross Depot at midnight. 'Goodbye, old tram!' he proclaimed, or (this being the 1950s) 'Goodbye old trem!'

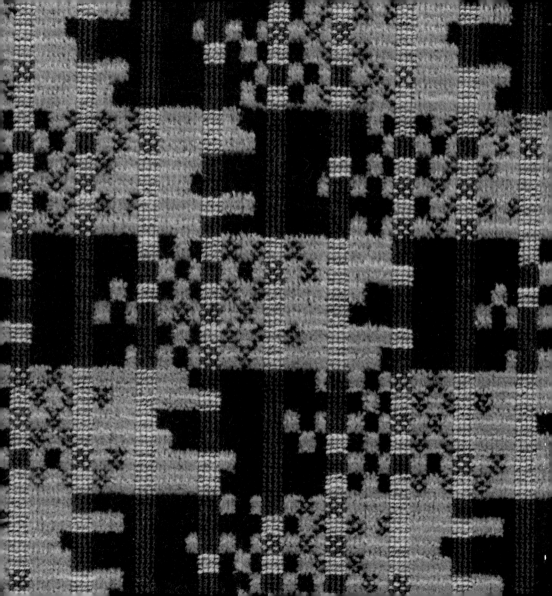

METROPOLITAN RAILWAY EXPERIMENTAL TRAIN 20000

In 1961, the Metropolitan's country line (the 'Extension Railway' as a rapidly declining band of fogeys call it) finally entered the 20th century, when the stretch from Rickmansworth to Amersham and Chesham was electrified. (Previously steam engines had hauled the trains.) The A-Stock trains (see p. 88) would be introduced in 1962 to coincide with the electrification, but they were the product of a long gestation period, during which the electrification beyond Rickmansworth had constantly been deferred.

A prototype train unfathomably numbered 20000 was built in 1946, and would run on the Met until 1956. It was different to the 1962 trains in several ways. For example, there were pairs of seats either side of a central gangway, whereas on the 1962s there were three seats on one side and two on the other. (Another prototype, numbered 17000, had been built with seats clustered in clumps of three down the middle of the carriage with gangways down either side, so nobody had a window seat. This prototype was then modified, and renumbered 17001, so that the seats were two on one side, three on the other, and this prototype became the model for the 1962 trains.)

But back to prototype 20000: this was its very attractive seat moquette. It seems leafy, countrified, and an advertising panel placed in the carriages of the prototype threw some light on the thinking involved: 'the interior has been designed to meet the varying needs of two distinct services: a country service to Amersham and a town service between Finchley Road and the City.'

The moquette is quite old-fashioned, but the Met seems to have been in nostalgic mood at the time, as we will see in the case of the next entry.

FOSSIL or TRILOBITE

To explain with scientific veracity what a trilobite is would require a great many words and the use of terms like 'arachnomorph arthropod', which doesn't get us very far. So: think, fossil of a spiral-shelled snail that died out 250 million years ago.

This moquette, known also as Fossil, created by Jack Thompson and Richard Eatough, was

used in 1958 on some mocked-up prototype interiors for what would become the 1962 stock, which would have open carriages, rather than compartments. It had also previously appeared on the Met's T-Stock trains, which would be displaced by the A-Stock and were electric multiple units (a modern notion) but with compartments (an old-fashioned notion).

Those compartments would have been made very cosy by the rich, lustrous greens and red of this moquette, which, in its darkness and use of organic forms, was consciously old-fashioned. As the Met relinquished its last steam engines, it was perhaps nostalgically recalling the glamorous late-Victorian days when it had aspired to be a mainline railway, and all its trains had first-class accommodation.

Trilobite can be seen in the London Transport Museum, in one of the compartments of the Metropolitan bogie stock carriage of 1900 vintage. This carriage had continued in service on the steam shuttle between Chalfont and Chesham until 1962. Having acquired the carriage (for £65), the Museum fitted out the compartments to show different time periods, and Trilobite is used in the one representing the 1950s.

'Trilobite was the last design to retain the spirit of that distinctive approach which had characterised Underground train interiors for 25 years,' wrote Paul Moss in *Underground Movement*, 'and therefore was the final legacy of the initiatives created by both Pick and Barman. The moquettes developed from the early 1960s onwards were plainer and more perfunctory in style and lacked the individuality and uniqueness of their predecessors.'

'POST OFFICE'

Just to get this out of the way . . . The 1959-Stock trains were introduced first on the Piccadilly Line, but would be dispersed pretty widely over the next forty years. The majority of the early ones would be put onto the Central (where they would be soon be replaced by the 1962-Stock), and the Bakerloo, where they would be displaced by the 1972 Mark 1-Stock, which is still there. When the 1973-Stock was introduced onto the Piccadilly Line, its 1959s were transferred to the Northern Line where they ran alongside the 1972 Mark 2-Stock.

'The new trains are lighter in weight,' proclaimed a poster, 'with an unpainted aluminium finish to save maintenance costs' (a rather downbeat message). The Silver (in Underground PR-speak; most people would say 'grey') harmonised with a progressive space-age aesthetic, but it presented – as would soon be proved – a blank canvas to graffiti artists. Internally, the cosiness of the 1938s was banished: these trains were bleak, with much grey plastic laminate and exposed fluorescent light tubes.

The moquette associated with the early 1959s, and subsequently rolled out the following year on the Metropolitan Line's new A-Stock, was similarly ascetic. (According to the London Transport Museum's own website, 'The attitude in the 1950s was that the people travelling on the trains would provide the colour'.) In his book *Underground Movement*, Paul Moss adjudged it

'effective but undistinguished'.

But it was the favourite moquette of David Holdsworth, scion of the main moquette-manufacturing company, Holdsworth's of Halifax. The moquette had been designed in house, and David worked on it in his early days at the family mill as a teenager learning the weaving trade. The complex pattern made it an interesting challenge to produce, and he liked the colours: 'a silver backing with black, and just a spot of Post Office red.' We will be returning to this moquette, and it will be convenient to give it a name, so I anoint it Post Office.

The Moquette Project

'You realise you've painted the top deck the wrong colour?' was the kind of thing the bus purists tended to say when they came on the heritage excursions organised by the London Transport Museum's Assistant Director of Collections and Engagement, Chris Nix. Understandably wanting to broaden the clientele on, for example, runs to Brighton on a Routemaster, he began taking samples of moquettes along, and found people were drawn in by them. It was about time, he began to think, the Museum gave moquette its due, by creating what he calls a 'moquette-opedia'.

In 2017 a Heritage Lottery Fund grant funded a year-long investigation, officially titled *Celebrating Britain's Transport Textile*, which became known as the Moquette Project.

The Project took its curator, Georgia Morley, to the Bluebell Railway, which has an upholstery department in its carriage workshop (an extremely restful place, smelling sweetly of wood shavings, with a radio playing quiet jazz and a resident cat flitting about); to the Victoria and Albert Museum, the National Railway Museum, and the London Bus Museum at Brooklands, where she worked closely with Nigel Fryatt, a volunteer curator assembling his own moquette display and database.

After years of being ignored, moquette suddenly seemed to be in the air. 'A lot more people are noticing it now,' says Georgia. 'In London it's partly because it's being sold at the LT Museum shop, but it's also because there are some very striking designs around at the moment.'

She mentions especially the work of Wallace Sewell, creators of the Barman moquette, which features London landmarks… but *which* London landmarks? The question is much Googled.

When Georgia (opposite) started out on the Project, TfL had 400 moquette samples in its possession, but in many cases no further information beyond a serial number. Her researches have attributed names, histories and designers to a lot of these mystery moquettes, and yielded some surprising revelations.

The iconic Roundel moquette, for example, had always been credited to a male designer, but Georgia discovered it was the work of an

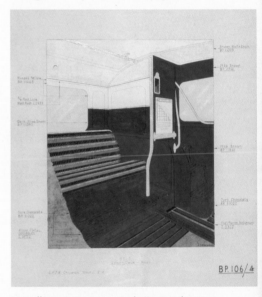

unsung female designer, Joy Jarvis. And who'd have thought that this extravagantly sensuous design from 1945 was not only by Enid Marx herself – it could not be more different from her usual measured, geometric style – but also, according to her letters to its commissioner, her favourite?

Just as there was an earlier golden age in the 1930s, so it's arguable that London Underground is currently in the middle of another golden age of moquette design. Where Enid Marx could speak of her favourite pattern as 'Paisley',

'Moorish' and 'Eastern', today's buzzwords are 'compliant' (with the Disability Discrimination Act), 'delivery', 'capacity' and 'consistency', but TfL's Head of Product Design Paul Marchant has commissioned some beautiful moquettes in the past decade and a half.

I hope this book will open people's eyes to them, and enable them to compare them to the moquettes of the previous 120 years. This would not have been possible without the work of Georgia Morley and her colleagues.

https://www.ltmuseum.co.uk/collections/projects-partnerships/moquette-project

ROUTEMASTER

The Routemaster hit the streets in 1959, a time when bus use was falling and car use was rising. In these straitened circumstances, buses had to be cheap, and the Routemaster, being of lightweight monocoque construction (no detachable chassis), was fuel-efficient while being able to carry eight more people than an RT.

Many Routemaster passengers would have possessed other subtly curvaceous products conceived by the bus's designer, Douglas Scott: one of his radio sets for Rediffusion perhaps, or his Aga cooker. And they would almost certainly have ridden in his previous bus, the RF single-decker, but it's unlikely they would have known Scott's name. He was a modest man, and he recalled that LT paid him for the RM 'out of petty cash', making the bus one of the great design bargains, like the Underground Map, for which LT paid Harry Beck approximately five guineas.

Its curved upper body and dimpled front makes the RM look smaller than it is. Soapy water flowed easily over those curves. 'London buses were kept in immaculate condition,' Jonathan Glancey severely notes in his book, *Douglas Scott*, 'until about 1970.'

The word for the bus interior is 'cosy'. Viewed from outside on a winter's night, it seemed like a welcoming lantern on the move, or a mellow pub with the conductor as landlord. The colour scheme was, officially, 'Burgundy lining panels, Chinese green window surrounds and Sung yellow

ceilings', the latter in anticipation of the colour that years of top-deck smoking would bring about anyway.

The moquette, designed by Scott himself, echoes this scheme with its red, green and yellow. It is possibly akin the dark tartan he had wanted to use for the linings of a luxury range of suitcases he had designed for Papworth Industries in 1947; but he had been required to use a brighter tartan instead. A set of the cases was presented to the ballet dancer Margot Fonteyn at the start of an American tour, and perhaps Scott was thinking of those luxury items in those graceful circumstances when he produced the Routemaster interior.

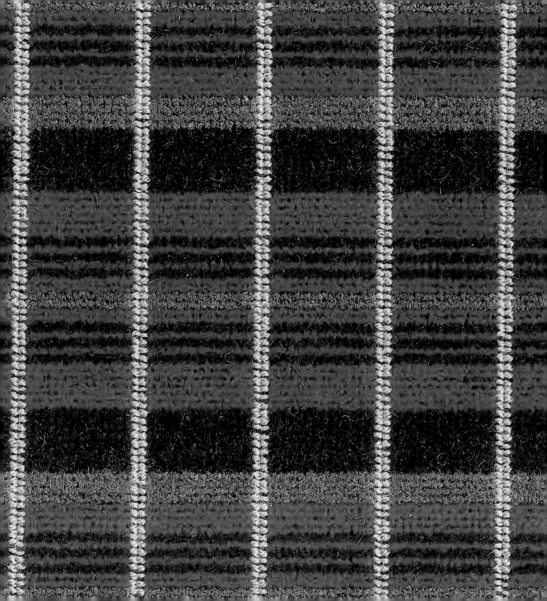

THE BACK OF WHICH MOQUETTE?

In fact it is the reverse of the Routemaster moquette on the previous page: this is what it looks like on the back.

Nothing like it, in other words – to a rather magnificent degree. As we saw earlier (see pp. 30-31), reverse Lozenge, on the other hand, was simply the Lozenge pattern – reversed.

If the fabric itself did not have the malleability of a thin carpet, requiring an industrial sewing machine to sew it together, this reverse-Routemaster would make an excellent waistcoat for a *boulevardier* sporting a Gitanes in a silver holder, or perhaps a whole suit for Graham Norton to wear on his chat show.

BEA

I can do no better than begin by quoting from an excellent website called *Old Bus Photos* (and believe me, it does what it says on the tin): 'From 6 October 1957 until 1 January 1974, British European Airways [in those days Britain's primary short-haul airline, with BOAC, British Overseas Airways Corporation, running the long-haul routes] operated a passenger transfer service between its West London Air Terminal at Cromwell Road, Kensington, and London [Heathrow] Airport. The rolling stock fleet was owned and operated by London Transport, and this was reflected in the vehicle types operated.' At first Regal coaches were used, but from 1964 rising demand prompted the use of adapted Routemasters (see next entry).

These Regal coaches were neither single-deckers not double-deckers, but rather, in the words of the Curator of the London Bus Museum at Brooklands, where one of them has been preserved, 'one-and-a-half-deckers'. It appears the passengers in the back half sat at a considerable elevation to those at the front. This would not have been for sightseeing purposes so much as to accommodate a large luggage compartment beneath them for all the suitcases.

The coaches were fitted with this attractively golden moquette. It must have been exciting to see it on the bus out to the airport – perhaps a little less so on the bus back.

GREEN LINE ROUTEMASTER

Routemasters were also available in green on Country Area and Green Line services. The coaches (RMCs and longer RCLs) were the most comfortable Routemasters: they had luggage racks, doors at the rear (rather than the standard open platform) to ensure warmth and safety on the longer and faster journeys like the 721 pictured here, from Brentwood to London Aldgate, and deeply cushioned seats intended to provide 'private car comfort'.

But the attempt to lure the ever-rising numbers of motorists out of their cars by using RCLs to compete with new, faster trains on BR Eastern Region was ill-fated. According to *Ian's Bus Stop*, the excellent website run by bus enthusiast Ian Smith, 'The RCLs should probably not have been built. Their market was rapidly disappearing at the time.'

No green was involved in this Green Line moquette – an acknowledgement perhaps that outer London was itself not as verdant as when the Green Line services had started. Rather its red, black and silvery grey colour scheme echoes that of the Post Office moquette that had made its debut on the 1962 Metropolitan A-Stock and would soon be on the Victoria Line. This moquette also appeared on Green Line RF-type single-deckers, and on the BEA Routemaster airport coaches.

These front-entrance Routemasters also had doors (BEA didn't want people falling off the bus as it sped down the M4 to Heathrow) and, from 1966, they towed trailers carrying luggage. Originally, the buses were liveried in cream and light blue, but, as the correspondent for *Old Bus Photos* notes, 'In 1969 the distressing vogue for the use of orange in buses gravely infected the BEA fleet.' Yes, they were painted *orange*. In 1973, when BEA merged with BOAC to form British Airways, the old livery was reinstated.

Dressed in your seat

Women – it is often said – do not like to turn up at an event to find another woman wearing the same outfit. (Neither – as is less often said – do men.)

Between 2008 and 2015, the German artist Menja Stevenson deliberately became a woman who finds herself, apparently by accident, wearing the same outfit as the bus or train she has just boarded. In short, she commissioned and then wore dresses made from seat fabrics. She started the project, which she called Bustour, in Stuttgart, then moved on to other German cities.

Generally, she didn't like the seat coverings. 'Why are they so ugly?' she wondered. One public transport official went some way to answering the question by telling her that the designs were conceived to 'turn off graffiti vandals', hence the use of as many shapes and colours in one pattern as possible. She wanted to draw attention to the coverings (which she thought most people ignored), to 'make the unseen seen', and another paradox follows, because she did this by 'camouflaging' herself, thereby – since a person

dressed as a seat could never be mistaken for a seat – becoming *more* rather than less visible.

Given the general lack of PR about the

seat coverings on public transport, it seems amazing that she was able to acquire enough of them to make the outfits, and she is proud of her achievement: 'I had to do a lot of persuasive effort . . .'

What was it like to wear the fabric?

'You sweat like crazy.'

Was that because it was wool?

'You are very lucky if you've got woollen fabrics in England. In my case, the fabrics had a fake velvet surface and were made of a certain dirt-repellent, Teflon-coated and extra-long-lasting high tech-fibre (as I was told).'

And what did her fellow passengers say?

'A few – very few – laughed, but most passengers would just look shyly at me, then quickly look away.'

Images from Bustour can be seen at **www.menjastevenson.de**. Menja also commends a website whose title translates as 'Seat Patterns of Death', **http://www.sitzmuserdestodes.com/galerie**

NEW LINE, OLD MOQUETTE

In the 1960s Britain belatedly embraced industrial design. A major commissioner was British Rail, for which Misha Black – the Russian-born co-founder of the Design Research Unit – had created a new livery known as Rail Blue. At the same time (early Sixties), Black was designing every aspect of the new Victoria Line, due to open at the end of the decade.

The Victoria was not an ambitious line: it did not open up any new part of London; its purpose was to provide a series of shortcuts across central London, and to that end, every station except Pimlico connects to another line. The line was intended to assist the London motorist by incentivising some other motorists to leave their cars at home.

It was built on the cheap. While Misha Black's 1967 Stock trains for the line – with the wraparound cab windscreens – are considered classics, the carriage interiors and the stations are not so highly regarded. The platforms are too small, and the platform tiles no bigger than domestic bathroom tiles, hence one satirist's definition of 'late lavatorial'.

The idea was to have a colour scheme based on whatever colour the Victoria would be allocated on the Tube map. Apparently, Black favoured a dark blue (he liked the 'Nanking Blue' of BR's luxury businessman's train, the Blue Pullman), but that would clash with the Piccadilly Line colour, so he settled on a pale

blue – Cambridge blue – which he combined with grey. Blue was a very Sixties colour, not occurring in nature (unless we consider that the sea and sky really are blue) and so suggesting the sophistication of a synthetic material.

And when it came to the moquette, the Victoria Line was even more of a compromise. Black had wanted a navy-blue-and-olive-green check designed by Marianne Straub (see next entry), which would have toned in nicely. But it wasn't ready in time for the line's opening in 1968. So Black had to make do with 'Post Office'. The mainly grey interiors of the trains – the first to have fluorescent light – appeared washed out, and the whole ambience of the line was described by the *Observer* as 'extraordinarily bleak'.

STRAUB

This is the moquette Misha Black wanted for the Victoria Line. It was designed by Swiss-born Marianne Straub, one of only three female designers of the 60-odd listed in *British Rail Designed 1948-97* by David Lawrence. She was prolific. In *A History of British Design 1830-1970*, Fiona MacCarthy notes that, in the late 1930s, Straub was 'designing for seventy Welsh textile mills'.

'Straub' first appeared on the Underground adorning seats – both transverse and longitudinal – of the new C69-Stock for the Circle, District and Hammersmith & City lines. More will be said about this stock when we come to consider its refurbishment in the early 1990s.

The moquette – for which Marianne Straub was paid 50 guineas – would be used widely on the Underground and buses over the next ten years. It was also used, in slightly simplified form – becoming a simple check in the same

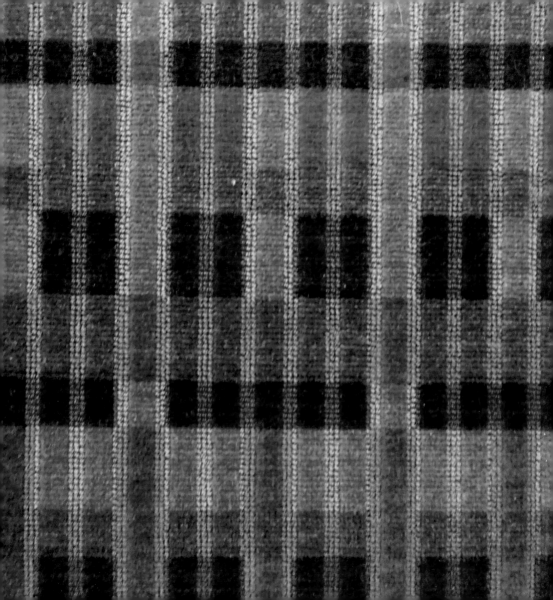

colours – on electric slam-door trains from Waterloo to the South Coast, where she matched it with orange curtains. This modified Straub seems to have been known as 'Bournemouth', after the destination of the some of the trains. Bournemouth was also applied to BR Mark 2 carriages in the Sixties and Seventies, and a more sober, charcoal-grey-and-black colourway was created for first class. In the opening credits of *Get Carter*, Michael Caine is sitting on grey-and-black Bournemouth, reading *Farewell My Lovely* in a first-class compartment of what was possibly the *Flying Scotsman*. He looks very demure for a man who will soon be throwing people off the upper levels of multi-storey car parks.

Straub was also used in the bleak interior of the Daimler Fleetline bus (see previous spread), introduced in 1971 as the follow-up to the Routemaster, and lacking its predecessor's dimpled charm, and the AEC Swift single-decker seen here. The DMS reflected glum

circumstances: falling London population, fewer bus journeys, LT staff shortages. With one-person operation now permitted, Fleetline passengers paid their fares either to the driver or by dropping the coins into an automatic turnstile. ('Think of it,' an LT advert said, 'as a phone box.')

'Something had gone horribly, horribly wrong,' wrote Travis Elborough in *The Bus We Loved*. 'Decimal currency had arrived, "Chirpy, Chirpy Cheep, Cheep" was riding high in the charts and now this: a London double-decker which had about as much charm and finesse as a Watney's Party Seven.' LT tried to make us love the Fleetline by imposing a nickname: 'The Londoner', but it didn't take and neither did the bus, which would be long outlasted by the Routemaster.

It was the fate of the subtle and sophisticated

Straub moquette (whose colours, like the sea, seem to fluctuate between predominantly green and predominantly blue) to be mismatched with its surroundings. If its sophistication was wasted on the Daimler Fleetline, it was too dour for the *Brighton Belle*, whose exuberant, jazzy moquettes had been replaced (in second class) by Straub in the late 1960s. 'The common or garden blue-and-green check moquette and bright orange curtains may have looked fine on a 4VEP [a slam-door electric train], wrote Stephen Grant and Simon Jeffs in *The Brighton Belle: a Much-Loved Train*, 'but did nothing for the art-deco splendour of the Belle.'

1938-STOCK RE-TRIM

This moquette was used to re-trim the 1938-stock Tube trains when they were given an EHO (Extra Heavy Overhaul) in 1977. By now, they were concentrated on the Bakerloo and East London Lines.

Between 1986 and 1988 five '38s were used on the Northern Line. I was a Northern Line regular at the time, and I used to spurn as many as two or three 1972-Stock trains in the hope that a '38 would turn up, because I so much preferred their interiors.

I think this was the moquette on them. It is also on the 1938 train at the Acton depot, and on the single 1938 carriage at the LT Museum, and yet the black-and-white photograph of an original 1938

interior, which stands outside this latter carriage, shows 'Leaf' by Marian Dorn, one of the classic moquettes commissioned for the 38s.

A curator told me the exhibited vehicles had been given this red and green check because it

was available and had the right colour scheme: it wouldn't have been worth commissioning another batch of one of the classics. 'Moquette is hideously expensive, and the minimum order is about 300 metres.'

This moquette is not a classic, but its functional check does use the essential colours of the classics: dark red and dark green, and so maintaining the 'serenity' Frank Pick sought for the '38s. Indeed, a curator at the LT Museum once told me, of the exhibited carriage, 'It's amazing how many people fall asleep in here.'

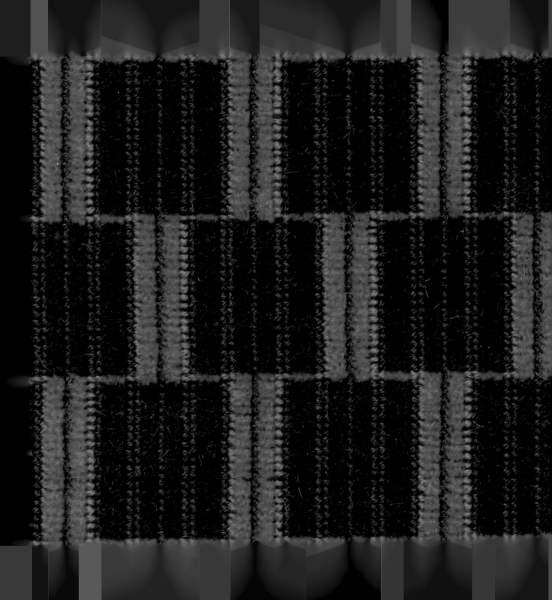

DISTRICT LINE D78-STOCK

This moquette, used on the D78 Stock trains that appeared on the District Line from 1980, emanated from Misha Black's Design Research Unit, and is usually attributed to Black himself, but according to the leading moquette designers

of today, Emma Sewell and Harriet Wallace-Jones (Wallace Sewell), it is by Jacqueline Groag, who worked for Black at the DRU. I myself was unsurprised to learn that it was not by Misha Black. He initiated a blue period that continues, in that blue remains the default colour of train or bus interiors, and this is a very un-blue moquette.

The LT Museum has produced a small book called *London Underground D Stock 1980-2017*. It describes the trains as providing a stark contrast to the 'dowdy greys and blues' of the C-Stock that preceded the D78s. The orange, yellow, brown and beige are warm colours, and the book underlines the point by showing a cushion made of the moquette placed next to a wood-burning stove. This moquette is the top-seller amongst LT Museum moquette products. It has become, according to the Museum's moquette catalogue, 'a subconscious icon of the city for 1980s residents and visitors.'

Affection for the moquette is possibly merged with affection for the old D78-Stock trains, which were slightly eccentric, with their single-leaf doors, with push-button operation ('The guard will not open the doors,' early publicity warned). You could have an entirely solipsistic journey: pushing the button to board the train alone; sitting in the single seat next to the door; pushing the button to leave.

The moquette would also be used on the Jubilee Line, and on the bus fleet's Leyland Titans and Metrobuses. I was looking at a display of this moquette in the LT Museum when a chap of about 50 came up with his young son. 'All the buses I took as a kid had that on the seats,' he said. 'It reminds me of going home from school on the 294, and all the girls from Frances Bardsley school taking the mickey out of my purple blazer.' I couldn't work out whether he was addressing his son or me, but then I realised he was actually speaking to himself, lost in the nostalgic reverie a moquette can so easily trigger.

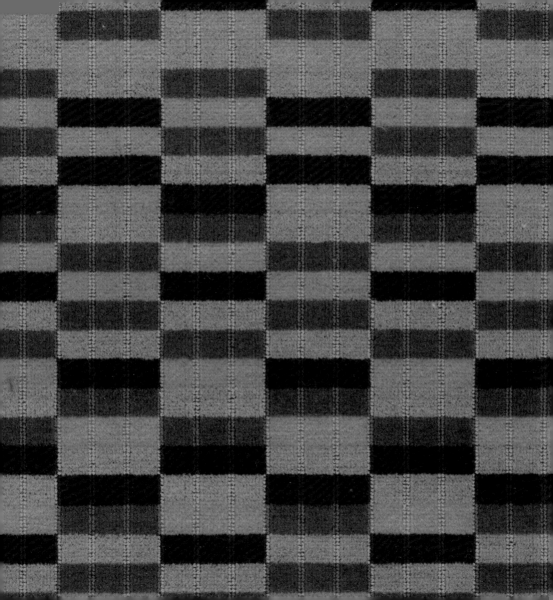

BLUE BLAZE

The Waterloo & City Line, known to its deprecators and friends (for some it does hold a morbid fascination) as 'the Drain', is an awkward footnote in the history of London Underground. It was built by the London & South Western Railway (a mainline railway) to take commuters from its terminus at Waterloo to the place they all really wanted to be: Bank, in the City. It was London's second Tube line, but it would not be part of London Underground until railway privatisation in 1994, a hundred years after its opening.

In 1993, this carriage was withdrawn from service, to be replaced by the 1992 stock, which was also used on the Central Line. It is preserved in its 1993 colours at the LT Museum's Acton depot. This means an external livery of chilly red, white and blue, the supposedly un-fusty colours of Network Southeast – an operational

sub-division of BR created in 1982. The moquette, called Blue Blaze, was used on many BR trains, and when it was applied to this carriage nobody seems to know.

The carriage was part of a set built in 1940 to the design of Oliver Bulleid, Chief Mechanical Engineer of the Southern Railway, tenants of Waterloo in those pre-BR days. The worm-like shape is reminiscent of an Electrolux vacuum cleaner, and it would have looked very modern at the time.

The interior of a Waterloo & City Line train is shown in *On The Beat*, a film of 1962 featuring Norman Wisdom as a bumbling (in fact, merely irritating) detective. The seat moquette is floral – I can say that much, but really nothing more, since the film is in black and white. Today, Waterloo & City trains have the ubiquitous Barman moquette (see later) whose blueness clashes with grab rails in the turquoise line colour.

THE GREEN TRAIN

In the mid-eighties, new stock was becoming due on the Central Line. The aim was to make a leap in Tube design, and the industrial design consultancy of David Carter, DCA Design, was invited to produce three subtly differentiated prototypes. The first was actually a reversion to earlier norms: the trains would have some colour on the outside. The A-Train was red; the B-Train blue; the C-Train green. All had externally hung doors, and radically lightweight bodies of extruded aluminium. They had bright interiors with large windows, a lot of white panelling, and grab rails instead of strap hangers. The vertical grab rails of the C-Train, Paul Moss writes in *Underground Movement*, 'were raked at an adventurous angle away from passengers standing in the aisles'. The effect was a bit like a book left lying on its back, the pages fanning out.

All the trains had moquette on the seats, but with 15 per cent nylon for greater durability; and on the green C-Train, the seats were harder than on the other two. The moquettes reflected the train colour, and that on the C-Train was a light, greenfly green, with a black pinstripe.

Of the three the C-Train was regarded as the most successful, which is partly why it's pictured here. The other reason is that the greenness of its interior is a throwback to the lost Pick-era notion of the 'serenity' of green. The C-Train would inform the design of the new Central Line trains, but not in terms of colour, and the greenness would be lost again.

A sample carriage of each train was exhibited in 1987 in a siding of suitably rangy Woodford station. In 1988, the trains ran on the Jubilee Line, both for testing and passenger-service purposes. A YouTube video also shows two of the carriages (blue and green) forming the shuttle train (Holborn to Aldwych) on the Aldwych branch of the Piccadilly Line. 'They look like something out of *Dr Who*', runs one of the comments – a backhanded compliment, possibly.

METROPOLITAN DIAMONDS

The 1962 A-Stock of the Metropolitan Line was refurbished throughout the 1990s. In anticipation of the walk-through S-Stocks that would be the next trains on the sub-surface lines, windows were put into the carriage ends. And this was the new moquette.

The dominant colour is magenta, the colour of the Metropolitan Line on the Tube map, and the pattern is known as 'Metropolitan Diamonds', a reference by the (unknown) designer to when today's Metropolitan Line was the Metropolitan Railway, that stubborn hold-out from the otherwise all-conquering Underground Group . . .

When, early in the 20th century, Frank Pick of the Underground Group was overseeing the development of the roundel, the Metropolitan declined to admit it to its own iconography, but it met Pick halfway. It would write its station names as they appear on the roundel: in white on a blue bar. This would not be backed by a red circle, however, but by a red diamond or rhombus.

According to Mark Ovenden in *London Underground by Design*, about 60 stations displayed the diamond, in particular Watford, Rickmansworth, Uxbridge, Farringdon and Aldgate. His book includes a photograph of the diamond at the station today called Great Portland Street, but verbosely known between 1923 and 1933 as 'Great Portland Street and Regent's Park', with the equally wordy footnote, displayed on the lower level of the signboard,

'For Oxford Street and Zoological Gardens'. In the latter years of its independent existence, the Met did allow the Johnston typeface onto some of its diamond signs, some of which persisted until the early 1970s, 40 years after the Met was swallowed up by London Transport.

Holdsworth and Co.

It's gratifying for us Yorkshiremen to note that there are still ways in which London is dependent on the North. The coal drops at King's Cross, which once received hundreds of tons of coal every day from the Yorkshire and Durham coalfields, may now be 'boutique retail', but the moquette on London's public transport is still made by West Yorkshire firms. The chief producer is Camira Fabrics, whose head office is located just outside Huddersfield (see pp. 18–19). But here we are concerned with Camira's predecessor, namely Holdsworth's of Halifax, which it acquired in 2007.

The last scion to run the firm, David Holdsworth, spoke to me by phone from his home in Halifax, which is presumably on the edge of town, and rather nice, since he was just about to go off horse riding, prior to a business trip to China. He's in the heavy-duty recycled rubber line these days.

David began working for the family firm as a teenager in the mid-60s, learning the weaving trade at the firm's Shaw Lodge Mill in downtown Halifax: he'd just left Harrow school and was about to go to Nottingham University. At school, he had enjoyed maths, physics, chemistry and rifle shooting. He 'did not enjoy history', which is odd, since he has created a very detailed and absorbing website (*story.theholdsworths.org.uk*) about the firm that for many years gave Londoners, as he put it, 'a good sit down'.

Holdsworth's began making moquette in 1903, when mechanised public transport was getting going. Prior to that, the firm (founded in 1832) had made damasks, tapestries, curtains and table covers. I had assumed that, whereas the availability of fast running water was no longer significant to the textile industry of Yorkshire, the close presence of a great many sheep *was*, but

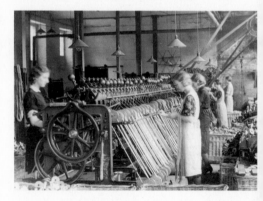

David told me, 'The wool for our moquettes was Merino from Australian sheep, which is very fine and soft. About one shearing was enough for a luxury coach seat or two Underground seats.'

It must have been strange, I suggested, working in Halifax, and not often seeing the moquette that you made in situ. 'No,' he said drily, 'but we saw enough of it – coming off the looms in the hundreds of yards.' He recalls that an inspector from London Transport used to come up to Halifax every few months, 'a Mr Peatfield, a lovely man. He'd check the rolls, and he would take a lead seal on a pink ribbon and clip it to the moquette with a pair of pliers.'

Much of the moquette made by Holdsworth's was designed by its in-house designers, people whose names have been lost to history. 'Ah,' said David, 'they didn't *have* names.' I asked him to elaborate. 'If it was known who'd designed a certain moquette they might have been headhunted by our rivals.' (Other moquette makers of West Yorkshire included Firth Furnishings and British Furtex.)

Today, Shaw Lodge Mill is in part a business complex accommodating many start-ups ('The Calder Valley is a very creative place,' says David), and what used to be the 'weaving shed' is given over to five indoor football pitches.

CENTRAL LINE CHECK

The gestation of the 1992 Central Line trains was, according to the designer Jonathan Sothcott, who had worked on the 1986 prototypes for DCA Design, 'amazingly long'. Mock-ups of the new trains were created by DCA, with a range of possible seat moquettes, and, Sothcott recalls, 'displayed to the Central Line public at Stratford station.' There was then a vote to see which moquette had customer 'buy-in'.

This design by Sothcott – Central Line Check – was the winner. He had been asked to produce a grid pattern, so that if the moquette were damaged it would be possible to cut out and replace a perfect rectangle. 'So there are lots of horizontals and vertical lines so you can choose where to cut. The colours are blue and red, which are the LU corporate colours, and the colour of the roundel, and then red is the colour of the Central Line itself. That red was a real gift – it's such a great colour.' (He would also use it for the grab rails, the first time they would have the line colour.)

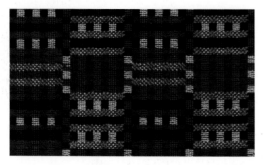

Below is one of the designs not chosen, by Susan Collier of the firm Collier-Campbell. Its plaid pattern seems elegant to me, but the 1992 trains marked the start of a rather territorial phase, when Tube interiors would reflect the line colours. Perhaps this design was found insufficiently red.

The winning design reflected Sothcott's interest in Op Art, 'in the sense that I wanted to make the colours vibrate – I hope not in a disturbing way. But you look first and you see a series of squares, but then you look again and you see stars or diagonals.'

The grey plastic armrests, incidentally, did not last long. They had 'frangible' joints, designed to break if people fell against them. 'Sadly this design detail was discovered by mentally challenged members of the public,' writes Paul Moss in *Underground Movement*, 'who promptly kicked the armrests into oblivion!'

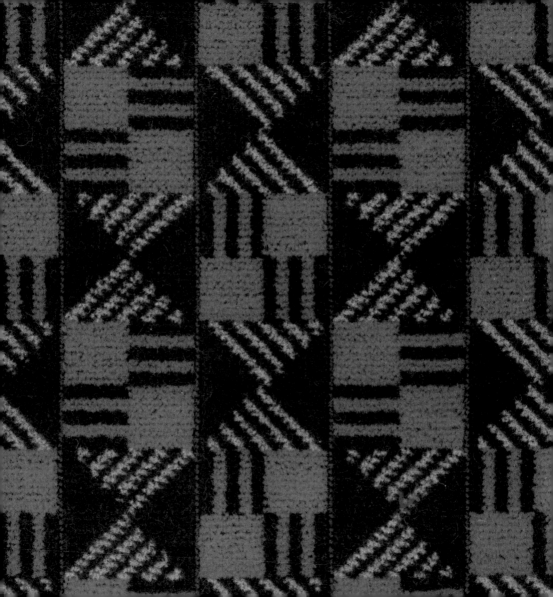

CROSSRAIL AERO

This was designed by Jonathan Sothcott, when he was working for DCA Design, for the planned Class 341 Crossrail trains, probably about the same time he was working on the Central Line moquette.

His memories of producing 'Aero' were a bit vague when he was interviewed in 2017 for the Moquette Project website, and he was surprised to see a sample of it presented to him. The Class 341s were intended for what was then merely the 'Crossrail project', and they are ghost trains, in the sense that they were never produced. Neither was this moquette, although a sample was woven.

'Well, it's very Eighties,' reflected Sothcott. 'Those swirls . . . the idea was that if the surface pattern seems broken up, it wouldn't show the dirt. I mean, if someone went at this with a Magic Marker, you might not be able to tell. It actually has the feel of graffiti itself. Yes . . . it reminds me of a shell suit, a real Eighties vibe.' He was sufficiently guarded on the subject for the interviewer to ask, 'Do you like it?' After a lengthy pause, Sothcott – a very straightforward man (probably because he's from Yorkshire) – said, 'I really liked the one I did for the Central Line.'

'EYES DOWN' or 'CRUSHED STRAWBERRY' or 'POACHED EGG'

This pretty charmless moquette was put on Routemaster buses when the remaining vehicles were refurbished in the 1990s, and remained in place until the bus was phased out in 2005. It replaced the red, green and gold cosiness of the original moquette, but was part of an attempt to create a lighter, brighter interior, along with fluorescent lighting. Against a mid-blue background, the moquette features some red blobs (hence the nickname 'Crushed Strawberry'); there are also white blobs within which is a smaller, orangey blob, hence the other nicknames for this moquette: 'Poached Egg' and 'Eyes Down'.

To soften the blow of the Routemaster's general decommissioning, some were retained on two so-called Heritage Routes, numbers 9 and 15, running alongside the longer scheduled services. At the time of writing, Routemasters only survive on route 15 (Trafalgar Square to Tower Bridge) and then only on weekends and Bank Holidays. The RMs on the route have this moquette, but your average Japanese tourist doesn't seem to mind. 'People love the bus just as it is,' a conductor on the number 15 told me in April 2019, and my journey was indeed very jolly. I was surrounded by a babble or babel of foreign voices, all speaking excitedly in praise (I assume) of the old bus.

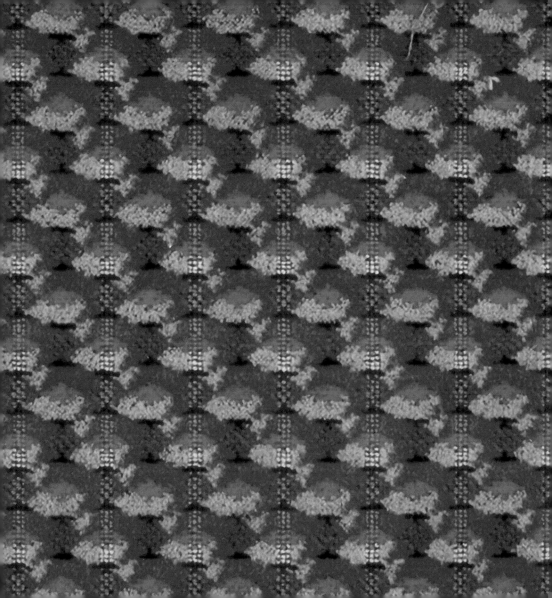

VICTORIA LINE 1967-STOCK REFURBISHMENT

The previously-mentioned 1986 prototypes, and the development of the 1992 stock, had the effect of making other Tube trains look dowdy. So in the late 1980s a programme of refurbishments began.

The first trains to benefit were the 1967s of the Victoria Line. These trains were stylish on the outside but had all the internal cosiness of a prison cell set up for suicide watch. The lighting was by bare fluorescent Tubes in the middle of the carriage, giving way to dingy gloom at the ends. The dangling, spring-loaded handgrips looked like coshes. The line diagrams were on panels that doubled as ventilation panels, and when these fell open they looked like shelves loaded with black dust. The advertising panels were illuminated but in practice, the space having not been sold, it was often a white void that was lit up.

The refurbishment saw the ceiling profile changed to allow glass luminaries to throw an even light. The grey panelling became a friendlier cream. The shape of the ventilation panels was changed so that they flowed with the new ceilings, and the advertising panels were re-coloured in blue, so that the absence of an advert might almost look deliberate. The maple wood floors – which had manifested as simply black, because of accumulated dirt – were replaced by a new 'slip-resistant' rubberised material in two shades of blue.

The old blue Straub moquette was replaced

by one reflecting the new exterior livery of red, white and blue. The aim was to create a moquette with the vigour and boldness of the 'classics' commissioned by Christian Barman in the 1930s, and the new one, designed by Pat Barrow of British Furtex Fabrics, has some of the intensity of a medieval tapestry. Since Frank Pick was once described as a 'mediaeval modernist', this is entirely appropriate.

C-STOCK REFURBISHMENT

By 1990, those Circle Line trundlers, the C Stock, had become uncongenial. They, like all the sub-surface trains, were plagued by graffiti artists who found them easier to get at than the deep-level Tubes. Like the 1967 Victoria Line trains, the C69s had too much grey laminate combined with filthy wood on the floor. There was too much crosswise clutter: transverse seats, bulkheads (panels stretching horizontally across the roof) and draught screens on either side of the doors created an effect of compartmentalisation, which (as Paul Moss genteelly puts it in *Underground Movement*) 'resulted in some unfortunate incidents concerning women passengers'.

Between 1990 and 1994, the Cs were refurbished. All seating became longitudinal; the bulkheads and draught screens were minimised, and windows were fitted at the carriage ends, so you could see into the next carriage, and possibly even the one beyond that – which anticipated the walk-through nature of the S-stocks that would eventually succeed the Cs. The reflective, ivory-coloured laminate that had brightened the 1967s was also introduced.

The new moquette was designed by Callow & Maddox. The effect was nocturnal: dark blue with a motif of three small squares arranged as the points of a triangle. They were maroon, yellow and green, and rather fuzzy, like distant electric lights seen through evening rain. The colours reflected the colours of the sub-surface lines: green, maroon and yellow. The pink of the Hammersmith & City line did not feature, either because that line was only given its own colour and separate designation on the map in 1990 (previously it had been shown as part of the Metropolitan), slightly too late to make an appearance on this moquette . . . or because pink just didn't go.

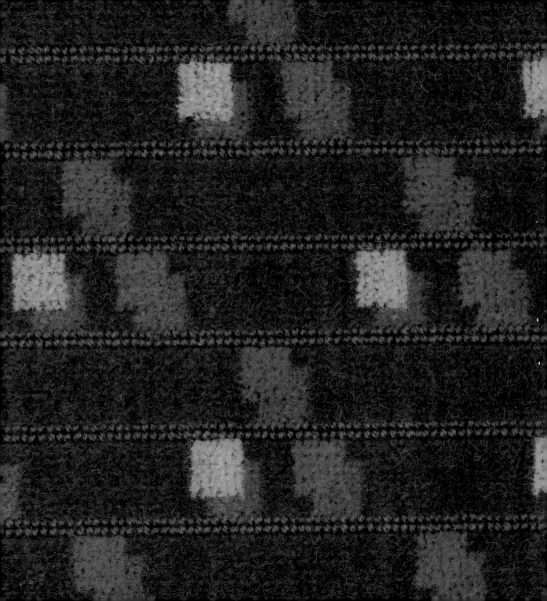

'ART DECO'

When the above-mentioned, and ill-fated, 1983-Stock was introduced to the Jubilee Line, the Bakerloo got the Jubilee's 1972 Mark 2-Stock, which at the time of the transfer had Straub moquette. In the early 1990s, these carriages were refurbished with this moquette by the firm of Jones-Garrard. Its name, Art Deco, is almost superfluous: you are put in mind of an inter-war cinema as soon as you look at it. It went well with the new, terracotta-hued armrests and grabrails, reflective of the line colour. (In the prototypes, the latter were ribbed, making them unfortunately suggestive of sex toys.) The 1972 trains were descendants of the 1938s, and the mellow shades of this refurbishment reflect that passenger-friendly tradition.

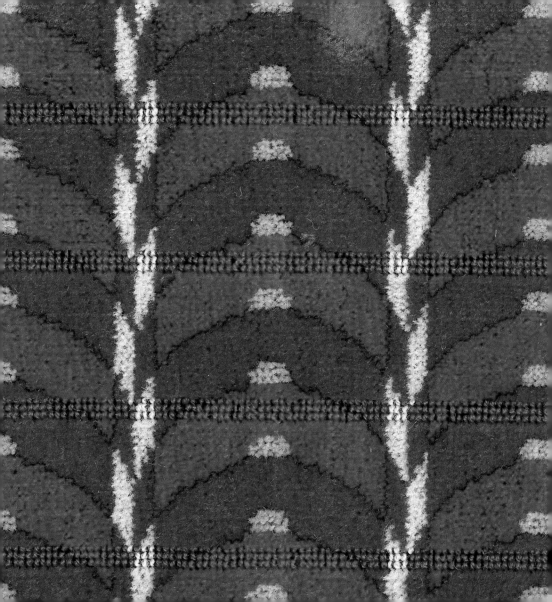

NORTHERN LINE 1972 AND 1959 STOCK REFURBISHMENT

This Deco-ish moquette – in orange, mauve, black and white, by Tinsley, Lumsden and Shane – is a rarity. It was used to refurbish four of the hundred or so Northern Line trains: one of 1959 stock, and three of 1972 Mark Is. It replaced, I think, either the Post Office moquette mentioned often above, whose colours it echoes, or Straub. I happened to show a picture of this moquette to Emma Sewell and Harriet Wallace-Jones of the design team Wallace Sewell (see several subsequent entries) and they liked its 'lovely flowing movement'. Jonathan Sothcott, designer of the new moquette for the Central Line at around the same time also remembers liking this one, 'although it was a bit blocky – like mine.'

I was a regular on the Northern Line in the mid-nineties, and I don't remember seeing this moquette. Then again, I was tending to look at the guards, who persisted on the Northern Line after the other lines had been lost to Driver Only Operation (DOO). I knew that the guards were about to be extinct, because new Northern Line trains were in the offing, and they would be DOO, hence my fascination. I used to admire their big, riveted leather shoulder bags, in which they usually carried a flask of tea and a book. In 1995, I wrote an article about the reading habits of guards. Here were some of my findings:

- *A pale, sepulchral guard: Interview with a Vampire by Anne Rice.*
- *A short, worried looking guard: London Underground Equipment Defect Log.*
- *A small, wiry guard: Lightning Strikes, by Gerald Souter (The Life and Times of Boxing's Lightweights).*
- *A long-haired guard: Rasp magazine, the cover of which featured a large cannabis leaf and headings such as 'Heavy Traffic', 'Dope Matters' and 'A Potted History'.*

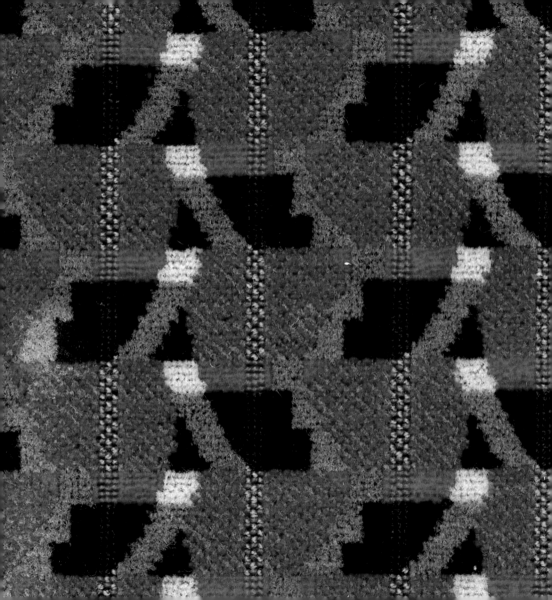

How do they do moquette abroad?

Paul Priestman, of the design firm Priestman Goode sees trains as 'culturally specific'. 'You need space for skis on Austrian trains . . . In Asia, people don't like to travel with their backs to the direction of travel.' A cultural characteristic of British trains – and London Underground trains especially – is that their seats have moquette coverings.

Some British trains and buses do have flat fabric (no pile, hence not moquette), but moquette is the norm, and has come to be expected on the Underground. 'It gives a warmth,' says Priestman, 'a London-ness . . . Certain cities can have soft furnishings, whereas in Hong Kong, for example, stainless steel seats are required. London is a cold and damp city, so stainless steel might seem a bit utilitarian.' But insofar as hard seats are provided to deter vandals, Priestman points out that moquette seats generate respect,

whereas 'if it looks like a prison, people will treat it like a prison.'

The industrial designer Ivan Bennett suggests another reason why moquette might be spurned. Moquette pile holds or grips the passenger in the seat, and this is needed in London and other European cities: 'They're medieval, with a twisting street pattern, and our Underground follows that pattern, with lots of dynamic movement. In South America, parts of North America and certainly Asia, you have more linear road-based railways.'

Nowhere else in Europe is as committed to moquette as London. To the left is moquette on a bus in Melbourne; above, plastic on one in Provence. In Germany or France, moquette might co-exist with vinyl or flat fabrics in wool or artificial fibres (see Menja Stevenson's Bustour

on pp. 102-3). On the Paris Metro, you will see moquette on some lines and polyester moquette (which has a shorter pile) on others; on the express RER lines, you see vinyl seats.

I love the Paris Metro, for its elegant white tiled stations (which have bevelled edges so they sparkle under electric light), its art nouveau station entrances and its general speed and efficiency. It is the latter quality that dictates my mental image of a Metro seat. I think of the *strapontin*, the folding or jump seats, which are more highly sprung than

their London equivalents, and I picture one of these banging back into the vertical position having been recently vacated by some purposeful Parisian. That London-style moquettes are not universally applied makes me think of Metro seats as temporary perches, whereas their London equivalents seem more like armchairs.

And what of the patterns themselves? How far are they culturally specific? Camira recently made this sumptuous floral moquette (left) for Paris, not London, and where could the fabulous striped pattern above, with its Fauvist colour palette, come from other than Paris?

JUBILEE LINE

The 1983 Jubilee trains (they of the lamented mustard-bath effect) were replaced by new trains, the 1996-Stock, which would serve a line in the process of being extended east to the fast-growing business district of Canary Wharf and on to Stratford. The new trains were similar to the 1992s of the Central Line, being of lightweight extruded aluminium and with externally hung doors. (They were also similar to the so-called 1995-Stock that would appear on the Northern Line in 1998.)

The original plan had been to refurbish the 1983-Stock, and Warwick Design Consultants, who had been working on that project, were retained for the new trains when it was decided to put the 1983s out of their misery. The colour theme of the carriages would be cream, aquamarine and purple. The moquette would be in those colours plus black. The plan for the grabrails would be that

they would match the line colour, a fetish that had started with the red rails of the 1992s on the Central. The line colour of the Jubilee was grey, or theoretically silver, to commemorate the year of the Silver Jubilee, in which it had opened.

So the plan for the grabrails was that they

would be stainless steel, but this made them evasive to the visually impaired. The Institute of Consumer Ergonomics in Loughborough recommended yellow (strictly speaking, 'grapefruit') as a more visible colour, and this was adopted. A yellow trace was also added to the geometrical moquette, in order to harmonise with the grabrails.

A further note on greyness . . . There would be a lot of it, either in the form of stainless steel or concrete, on the stations of the Extension. Those stations were popular with the public, but, as Mike Ashworth, Design and Heritage Manager for TfL, told me in an interview conducted a few years later, 'After the opening of the Extension, there was a big kickback against the grey: people wanted more colour.'

YELLOW PAGES

The London Underground bombards the traveller with advertising from the moment you swipe your Oyster card: ads as you ride down the escalator, ads on and opposite the platform, ads above the seats inside the carriages. But actually *sitting* on an advertisement woven out of moquette is quite rare. To date there have been (someone will doubtless write in to correct this bold claim) three instances.

Far and away the most arresting was the Yellow Pages moquette that adorned a Circle Line carriage from 1995 to 2001. For the benefit of the Google generation, let me explain that this was originally a vast paperback phone book you consulted for the phone numbers of business and tradespeople: in those distant days if you needed your toilet fixed you didn't go on Checkatrade. com: you looked in Yellow Pages. For a while it had a slogan that went, 'Let your fingers do the walking,' which some found hilarious. This moquette, the lurid mustard yellow aside, maintains a greater sobriety.

The only two other instances seem to have been a plain, but dazzling, moquette in fuchsia pink to herald the digital switchover, and a red moquette that appeared on the Waterloo & City Line to advertise the Rugby World Cup. It would be interesting to know how far the rarity of such moquette-based campaigns is because the intended consumer is not expected to obscure the message by literally sitting on it.

LERS CHARITY SHOPS

ES ESTATE AGENTS

PNOTHERAPISTS TE

KARAOKE KARTING

TELEPHONES NEWSAG

CES QUANTITY SURVE

LICITORS SQUASH C

NG SERVICES UMBRE

YACHT EQUI

DLR

The Docklands Light Railway was opened in 1987. One of its westerly prongs, from Tower Gateway to Westferry, runs over the route of the old London & Blackwall Railway, which at first had its London terminus at Minories, close to the current Tower Gateway DLR station, before being extended to Fenchurch Street. 'Those frequent and quite empty trains of the Blackwall Railway ran from a special platform at Fenchurch Street,' wrote John Betjeman in *First and Last Loves* (1952):

> *I remember them. Like Stagecoaches they rumbled past East End chimney pots, wharves and shipping stopping at empty black stations till they came to a halt at Blackwall station… where there was nothing to see beyond it but a cobbled quay and a vast stretch of wind-whipped water.*

This moquette, introduced during a 2002 refurbishment, seems to show that wind-whipped water, and reflects the wave pattern depicted on the sides of the trains. Judging by an internet

film called *Docklands Light Railway Comes to Stratford*, shot on the line's opening day with a retro newsreel-type score, the previous moquette had been dark blue with black checks. But I am going on the briefest glimpse, the moquette, as usual, being regarded by the film maker as of no importance. This new one was part of a process of aligning the DLR graphically with TfL – hitherto it had not had the Johnston typeface or roundel.

The moquette seems a bit lame: the waves are too spaced out. It has, I think, been recoloured since, because the red wavelets seem shorter and the yellow have become white. But if any trains can be excused a mediocre moquette it's the DLR's, from which the views of old and new East London jostling together give a sense of timeslip, and the sky always seems to be doing something interesting. An early poster for the DLR urged Londoners to 'catch the Light', and you do indeed.

OLD METROPOLITAN

The name is appropriate, in that this moquette was the last to be applied to the A-Stock trains on the Metropolitan before they were replaced by the S-Stocks of 2010 – and in 2003 the A-Stocks *were* old (41, to be exact).

Here, triangles replace the diamonds of the previous Met moquette. The majority of the triangles are in the Met's colour (magenta), but it is harder to connect triangles to Met Line iconography than it had been to connect diamonds. I can think of only one Metropolitan triangle: the pediment that topped off the pompous *porte-cochère* built onto the front of Baker Street station when it was remodelled in 1924. Inside the pediment was a clock and the words 'Baker St. Station'.

In 1927, the Metropolitan Railway exploited its air rights by building a block of luxury flats, Chiltern Court, on top of the station. Chiltern Court attracted rail enthusiasts, in that the flats to the rear overlooked the cutting from which Met trains began their journeys north along the 'extension line' to Amersham and Chesham. Hughie Green, the quiz-show host, lived in Chiltern Court and had a model railway in his flat. H. G. Wells, who often wrote about railways, also lived in Chiltern Court. The *porte-cochère* is long gone; the flats survive, although what had been their restaurant is now a Wetherspoon's.

DISTRICT LINE REFURBISHMENT

The District Line trains were refurbished in 2005. They ceased to be silver (so that was the end of an era). The new corporate livery of white, red and blue was applied with vinyl stickers; windows were cut into the carriage ends, and the ball-end strap hangers (the things that looked like dangling coshes) were replaced with straps.

The question of what moquette to use had been mulled over for an exceptionally long time: since 1996, in fact. The classic, turmeric-hued D78 moquette was becoming worn-out but, as Paul Moss writes in Underground Movement, it was 'a hard act to follow'.

Below are two proposals that were eventually rejected. They look smart enough to me. If the one on the right had been applied, I would have enjoyed trying to discern the squares and chevrons made up from the triangles. Triangles seemed to be fashionable at the time, because a triangular-patterned moquette had recently been be applied to the Metropolitan Line A-Stock trains. (See previous entry.) But perhaps these were considered too severe: it would be like sitting on sharp objects.

On the opposite page is the moquette that won out. Like the others, it is predominantly blue and green (green being the District's line colour), but darker, more abstracted and generally self-effacing – perhaps too much so. Although I'm often on the District Line, I have no memory of this moquette.

CAFÉ

The London Transport Museum was rebuilt in 2007, and it re-opened with a new café called the Upper Deck. It was decided to cover a bank of seats with this moquette, an adaptation of the fabled District Line one of 1978: 'A new colour combination of red and three green shades was chosen,' was the official explanation, 'to express the tranquillity of the space and the freshness of the café menu.'

I visited the café to conduct a vox pop. 'This is a moquette,' I said to a group of four people – three men and a woman. 'Do you like it?'

They looked at it, and, gradually – perhaps a little dutifully – agreed that they did.

It turned out they were German, from Augsburg, near Munich. 'We're bus drivers,' said one of the men, indicating the other two – 'and she's a tram driver.' So it was literally a busman's holiday.

'Do you have moquette in Germany?' I asked.

'No, not really,' said the spokesman.

'Then what are your seats covered with?'

They all got out their phones, and showed me photographs of various bus or tram seats.

'You see, they are not padded,' said the spokesman.

'And what is the material?' Is it wool?'

'Yes, but not from an animal.'

'A man-made fibre, then?'

'Yes.'

'Is the bus driver's seat covered with the same

stuff?'

'Oh, no, the driver's seat is much better.'

And the spokesman showed me a thickly cushioned, probably leather, seat with a headrest, armrests, and various levers for optimising comfort.

'What do you think of London buses?'

'We like them,' all three bus drivers chorused.

I asked why.

'Because they are a nice colour and they are double-deckers. I would like to drive a double decker,' said the spokesman. 'Although I would have to be careful when going through tunnels.'

So I told him the story of the Blackwall Tunnel STLs.

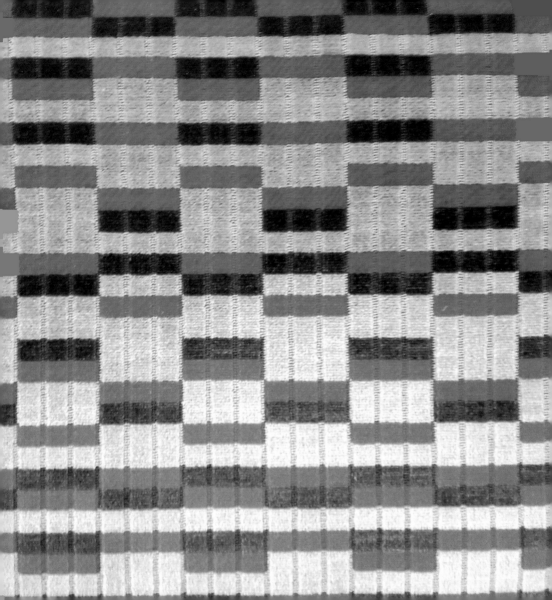

Moquette in your living room

In 2007, Mike Walton, then Head of Trading at the London Transport Museum, decided to start selling things made of moquette. I asked him why.

'Gut,' said Mike. 'It's the psychology. There's something about moquette – especially if you were well-disposed to the patterns – that kicks off memories. If you were using public transport, you were using it for an important purpose: school, work, hospital appointment, whatever – so the memories tend to be important.'

Of course, memory does not play a part in the case of some someone who buys a cushion, an upholstered stool (I call them pouffes) or a chair in the moquette called Pimlico, which was originally used on the Edwardian B-Type bus. Nobody remembers riding on a B-Type.

'Ah,' says Laura Mullins, Mike Walton's successor as head of trading, 'but we do have our enthusiasts, and they know exactly what they're buying.'

The moquettes sell mainly to the domestic market. 'Foreigners,' says Laura, 'are more interested in the roundel and the map,' which, presumably, is because they have not done their time on the Tubes or buses. The moquette has always sold well. 'It's the shop's USP,' says Laura (and it should be added that the shop is the only place from which, for copyright reasons, TfL moquette *can* be bought).

In 1997, I wrote an article for the *Evening Standard* about how the iconography of London Transport, as available from the Museum shop, was selling well amongst the fashionable young – T-shirts featuring the roundel, Harry Beck's Tube map or 'Mind the Gap'; a 'babe vest' inscribed 'Angel'; boxer shots featuring slogans such as (in ascending order of lewdness) 'Open flap for Ventilation', 'Hold Tight', 'Stand on the Right'. These appealed, I suggested, to the slightly ironic patriotism that was an element of the Cool Britannia/Britpop phase.

Today, a related irony operates: the extreme functionalism of moquette chimes in with the workmen's jackets and artisan stylings of the hipster generation. Laura recalls one customer: 'He had the beard, the tote bag, and he was looking at the socks with moquette patterns. I thought: of

course – because he wears his trousers rolled up. . .'

Number one on Laura's list of the 30 available moquettes ranked in order of sales is the orangey District Line 1978-Stock; second is the classic Routemaster tartan. Both date from periods sufficiently far back to generate nostalgia, and the D78 moquette has become something of a cult, famous for being famous. It also hits the right demographic: people who experienced it during their formative years are now at the height of their earning power. (The Museum retails moquette-covered sofas at nearly £2,000, 'and they *do* sell,' says Laura.)

The top two are also warm colours, and I think that is significant. I once asked a man (a rail enthusiast) who had returned to London after years living abroad to distil the essence of a nostalgia for the Underground. 'It's about being warm and cosy underground,' he said, 'when it's cold and rainy in the streets above.' Moquette is the main contributor to that.

'TUBE LINES'

This moquette dates from a 2007 refurbishment of the 1973-Stock Piccadilly Line trains. It is still on most of them, although in 2018 two were re-upholstered with Barman (see pp. 164-5) when temporarily given the 'Free the Night' livery, depicting a starry sky, to advertise the Night Tube, presumably because this 2007 moquette doesn't suggest any kind of freedom, but rather commuter drudgery. Twelve years on from its installation, it looks baggy and worn, surely giving a bad impression to visitors newly arrived in London and boarding at Heathrow.

The moquette detracts from the (admittedly antiquated) virtues of the 1973-Stock trains, which represent a honing by Misha Black and the Design Research Unit of their sleek Victoria Line trains. 'The full beauty of the design can best be seen on the long surface runs out to Heathrow,' observed Martin Pawley in the *Architect's Journal* in 1987, 'where the trains touch 60mph and their big,

automobile-style wraparound windscreens, long cars and low, tunnel-fitting profile and natural aluminium finish still lend them the electric excitement of the prototype – a decade after the line was opened.'

On the other hand, that very droll website *The Londonist* observed of this moquette, whose designer is unknown, that it looks like 'a twelve-year-old boy's bedroom curtains in the mid-90s.'

OVERGROUND

The old North London Line between Richmond and Woolwich became such a byword for crime, vandalism and railway bleakness that in 1997 it was re-christened the Silverlink Metro.

A less cosmetic makeover in 2007 saw the line taken over by TfL and, together with various other bits of Victorian railway meandering around London, brilliantly conceptualised as the London Overground. The network was given its own line colour: orange, last seen as the colour of the East London Line (the only Tube line wholly outside Zone 1), which now makes up the eastern segment, despite being partly underground.

Harriet Wallace-Jones and Emma Sewell, who met at the Royal College of Art and trade as Wallace Sewell, were one of five companies approached by TfL to propose moquette designs for the Overground. Their winning entry was of a throw called Chenille they'd made earlier (see p. 157), which was – and is – for sale in their shop in Islington. The pattern, featuring horizontal rectangles, would influence the design of later moquettes, by Wallace Sewell and others. It was

influenced by Bauhaus principles, Emma Sewell explained to me, in being 'geometric and abstract'.

Wallace Sewell turned out to be good at moquettes, and are highly rated by Paul Marchant, Head of Product Design at TfL. They relished the standard moquette-making discipline of having to use only four colours: in this case, two greys, brown and orange. They made the number look greater by pixilating the grey over the brown in certain squares, each pixilation formed of a single uncut tuft or loop of wool.

This cheerful yet elegant moquette has helped the Overground gain its salubrious image as 'the hipster line'. In February 2018, ten weeks after the Overground began offering night trains at weekends, it was reported that only a single nocturnal incident had occurred: the theft of a bag from a passenger who had fallen asleep.

Wallace Sewell

Wallace Sewell sounds like a stylish, but overlooked, novelist of the 1930s. In fact, it denotes Emma Sewell and Harriet Wallace-Jones, the leading designers of London transport moquettes over the past decade. They don't just make moquettes; they produce a range of woven products which are casually heaped up in every corner of their small premises in Islington, an ex-corner shop in which too much colour seems to have been packed into too small a space.

Wallace Sewell are not allowed to sell their moquettes in the shop for copyright reasons, but some of them are lying about, and they seem to make a double impression. In this highly decorative context, they look like what they are: sophisticated works of art – which is not quite how they are intended to appear when placed on the trains. 'Moquette is utilitarian,' says Harriet Wallace-Jones: 'in a way you shouldn't even notice it.' (She once observed, in another interview, that 'Nobody goes to the theatre and

says, "I love these seats."') On the other hand, the moquettes on show appear out of place, these designs seeming to belong in a more public context. It's as if you'd walked into the shop to be confronted by the statue of Eros.

According to Emma, 'Some of our customers don't know we do moquettes; when they see them, they're surprised, and then they start reminiscing about journeys.'

Wallace Sewell don't only have their own moquettes (Overground; Croydon Tramlink; the two Crossrail ones, and the ubiquitous Barman) in the shop: they also have some classics produced by others, including Marion Straub's richly blue and green moquette that takes her surname, and which seemed to be on every other bus and Tube in the 1970s. Wallace Sewell keep it to hand, I suppose, in much the same way that any pop musician would have a Beatles album lying about.

Harriet passed the Straub over to me, inviting me to feel the texture: the pile is both cut and uncut, so there is a tactile complexity to it that ought to be appreciated. there is also a visual difference between cut and uncut pile, Emma explained: where it is cut, the colour is more intense. Such 'tricks' are useful in moquette design, to give the impression that there are more than the standard four colours involved. (The Wallace Sewell motto, incidentally, is, 'Take four colours; make it work; make it beautiful.')

There were two other Wallace Sewell staffers in the shop: both women. It is inescapable that

moquette-making is a primarily female art, arising as it does from the domestic context. I own a book by David Lawrence called *British Rail Designed 1947-1997*. Of the 80 or so designers listed in the index, four are women; two of those are moquette designers, and one is a clothes designer. 'Even at the Bauhaus,' Emma Sewell told me, 'the women tended to do the weaving.'

('Even' because the Bauhaus was supposedly progressive.)

Wallace Sewell speak often about the Bauhaus: its influence is there in most of their moquettes, in that they are abstract and geometric . . . Not in the all-conquering Barman though, which is partly figurative in its representation of London landmarks. Emma, who originated Barman, says, 'I was influenced there by Russian Constructivism: the way that a tractor, say, might be represented in those designs.'

When I stepped out of the shop at the end of the interview, the street looked very grey indeed after the profoundly colourful world of Wallace Sewell.

TRAMLINK

In 2008, TfL took over the Croydon trams, officially known (presumably the word 'tram' is seen as too perfunctory) as Tramlink, which opened in 2000, providing the first trams in London since 1952. No slatted seats on top this time: these trams are single-deck.

In 2008, the trams, hitherto a rather attractive (and traditional) red, were re-coloured in green and cream, which is also attractive. Wallace Sewell were commissioned to do the moquette. The stipulated colour palette involved our old friends red and green, so often called in when London Transport wanted to suggest town-meets-country. (As Harriet Wallace-Jones said to me, 'Croydon *is* in the countryside – sort of.') TfL also wanted to emphasise that you can connect to the tram at Wimbledon Underground station, which is on the District Line, which is green. (The line diagram has an endearing little green bar underneath 'Wimbledon' with 'TRAMS' in small capitals.)

Wallace Sewell wanted to use 'the lovely olive green you see for the District Line on the old Tube maps', but a brighter green was required, which is a shame: there's a kind of unripeness, or extreme newness, about the Croydon Tramlink green, especially as used on the grabrails. Wallace Sewell's moquette is subtle nonetheless, and interestingly involved. The last time I was on the Croydon tram, I spent a lot of time trying to work out the repeat and pin down the colours. It wasn't easy. Wallace Sewell explained some of the games they'd played: for example running the red over the green, which makes the red seem like orange.

When the Croydon trams are running past back gardens, as they do for much of the time, you feel you're riding on something that ought properly to have the designation Light Rail (which comes from 1970s America). But in central Croydon, running alongside cars, you feel you've gone back in time, and are riding on a proper London tram, especially on a rainy night as you pass illuminated Victorian pubs.

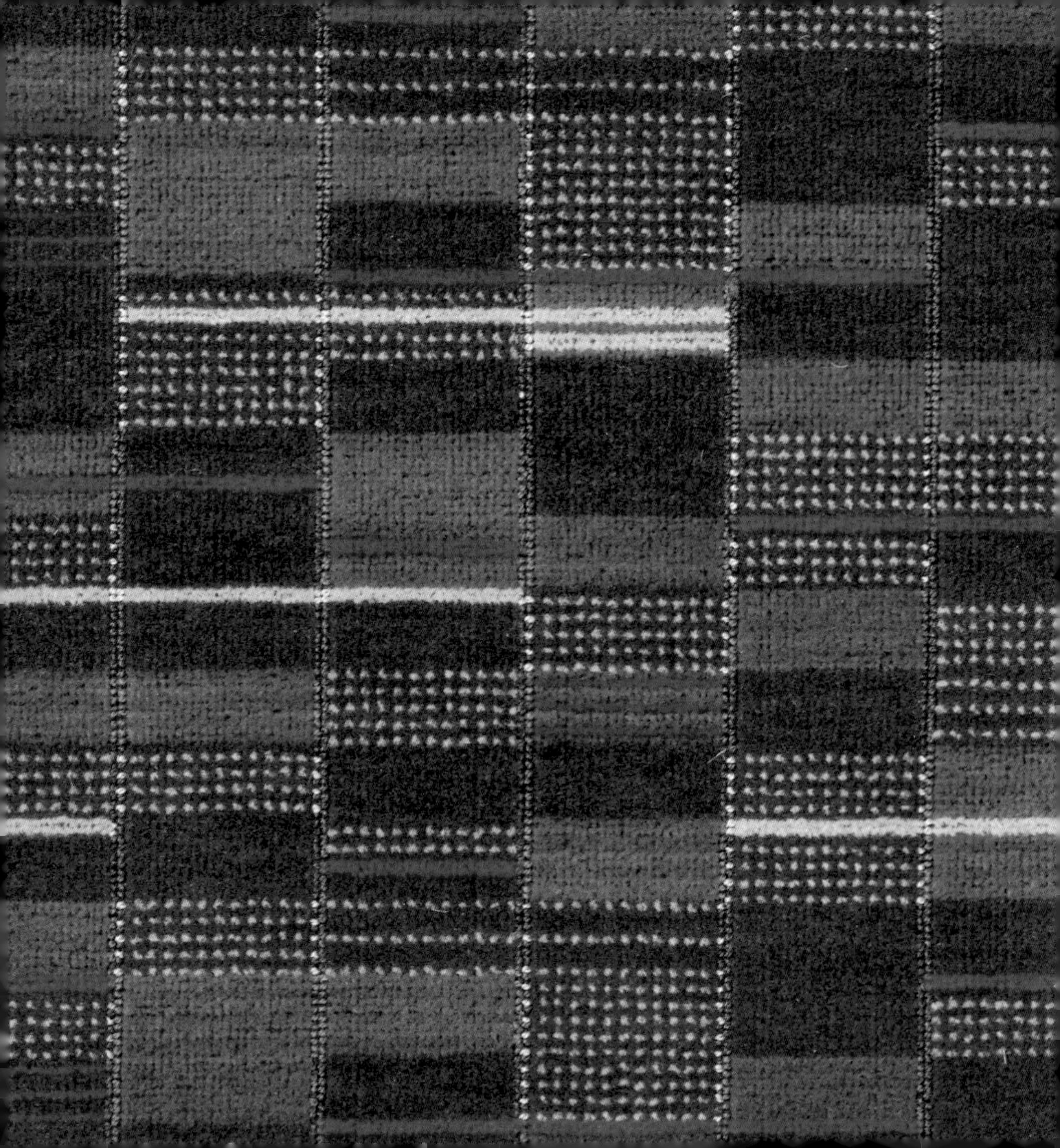

VICTORIA LINE 'NOUGHTS AND CROSSES'

The trains that replaced the 1967 Stock on the Victoria Line are the widest Tube trains on the Underground, the loading gauge (the tunnel clearances) being slightly wider than on the other lines. The 1967s didn't take advantage of this; the 2009's do. They are one and a half inches wider.

The trains have a pleasantly bright interior, partly thanks to this moquette, which takes its cue from the moquette that appeared on the line back in 1988. There are the same intersecting, sideways Vs, denoting she who was not amused. This new one is perhaps even more regal, the red dots suggesting jewels. It features light and dark blue, perhaps too much of the former (which is the line's colour), and also too much white: it shows the dirt.

Nevertheless, I find the Victoria Line trains slightly claustrophobic. The wideness is squandered by a steepling effect, the carriage sides pinched together at the top. But this impression is no doubt informed by my awareness that the line is entirely underground. That's true of the Waterloo & City Line as well, but I don't often travel on that. The Victoria is a bit less subterranean than the Waterloo & City, since there's an open-air depot at Northumberland Park, but that's for trains not people.

I regard most Tube lines as being like escape tunnels: sooner or later, you will emerge, triumphantly, in the open air, and it always seems to be sunny when that happens. Not on the Vic.

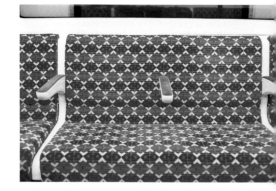

I am particularly conscious of this on hot summer days, when, as I descend towards the trains at Green Park, I walk past a series of giant electrical fans painted in the line's colour and attempting to ward off the heat in – it seems to me – a desperate, flailing way.

S7 and S8 STOCK

For those of us who try to comprehend London Underground rolling stock, the S Stock, introduced onto the District, Metropolitan, Hammersmith & City and Circle Lines in 2010, came as a pleasant change. It was so simple: one stock for the four most complicated lines (one of which, the Circle, is not actually a line but a route). The complexity of the lines, and of the Met in particular, helps account for the diversity of stock that has been used. Working its way through the alphabet, the District Line had reached N Stock by 1935, and none of those letters stood for anything, whereas in the present case S stands, helpfully enough, for sub-surface. (This stock, by the way, is not to be confused with the S Stock that appeared on the Metropolitan Railway in 1919, a designation applied, as far as I can tell, to a single eight-car train.)

The S7s are seven-car trains for the Circle, District, Hammersmith & City; the S8s are eight-car trains for the Met – so the numbers are also comprehensible. The S Stocks on the Metropolitan Line have some transverse seats, fitting for a line that runs out into the proper countryside. (On a transverse seat, you only have to move your head slightly to take in the view; on longitudinal seats, you have to crane right round.) Another retro feature is the strap hangers, which were fitted to the grab rails when it was found the latter were too high.

The trains seem spacious and light; they are

walk-through and air-conditioned, which cannot be said of any other Tube trains so far. The elemental nature of things is compounded in that the S Stocks have a single moquette. It takes its cue from the last one on to appear on one of the stocks the Ss displaced, the C69, in that it is a nocturne: small rectangles in the colours of the sub-surface lines are paired against a dark background, and the darkness leaks through between the colours, as with liquorice all-sorts.

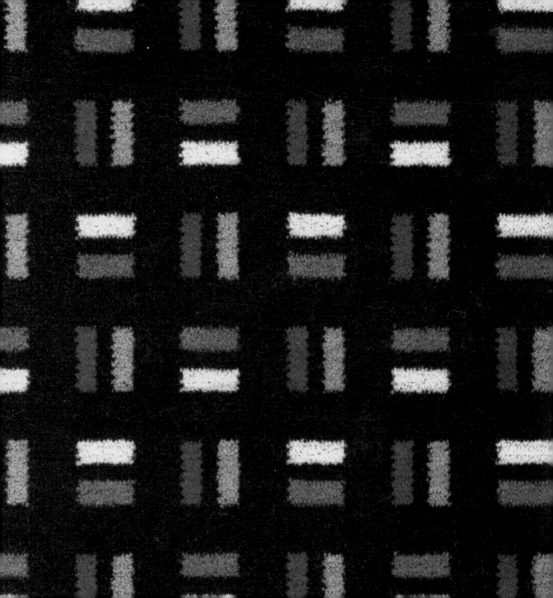

BARMAN

As readers of this book may have noticed, Tube moquettes were becoming rather diffuse, a different one being applied to every new refurbishment. There was a growing mood in favour of more uniformity, so TfL held a competition to find an elemental new London moquette that would reflect 'the spirit of London'.

There were 300 entries from around the world, including four from Emma Sewell and Harriet Wallace-Jones. Three of theirs made the top four, including this, the overall winner (and I stress this was a blind competition, with no favourites shown by TfL to previous clients). Wallace Sewell had called the winning design 'Landmark', but it was later re-christened in honour of Christian Barman, who, as Frank Pick's right-hand man, had commissioned those classic moquettes of the 1930s.

There are only four colours, but one of them – red – is pixilated in places against the blue to suggest a fifth. Barman is a grid, with each of the squares accommodating a London landmark. 'I sketched some buildings from memory,' recalls Emma Sewell. 'There's London Bridge, the London Eye, the dome of St Paul's, Big Ben . . . and Harriet always claims to see Battersea Power Station, but I don't remember putting that in. The dark blue is 'Piccadilly Line blue', and the red of the London Eye is 'more or less' the corporate red' of TfL, as seen on the circles of the roundel.

This moquette was originally intended for the Piccadilly Line, but (except for a couple of trains: see pp. 152-3) that turned out to be one of the few Tube lines Barman would not conquer. Its actual debut was on the Central Line.

EMIRATES AIR LINE

The Emirates Air Line, which opened in 2012, is a punningly-titled cable car sponsored by the eponymous airline and operated by TfL. In spite of that sponsorship, the taxpayer contributed about the half the £60 million cost. In crossing the river from North Greenwich to Royal Victoria docks, it connects two places that did not seem desperate to be connected, and on the two occasions when I have used it, I have been the only person peeling away from the Royal Victoria DLR station for the five-minute walk to the cable car. (You don't know whether to tap out with your Oyster card or not.)

The ride is beautiful, though, which is why I have done it twice – both times in the early evening with the sun descending over the West End like the upper half of an LT roundel, and the red illuminated batons on the fronts of the cars glowing in the descending gloom. Down below, that serpentine kink in the river – hard to comprehend at ground level – is made suddenly explicable.

The whole thing is mesmerisingly silent, and I entertained the sci-fi fancy that these illuminated batons were the actual power source of a series of flying pods.

The two bench seats in each car have a pretty moquette comprising rectangles in four shades of red, like a wall made of variegated bricks.

Perhaps this sense of a floating bubble gave someone the idea of offering a service of champagne in certain cars on Thursday and Fridays after 5, and after 12 at weekends. It revives some of the indulgence of two luxury Pullman cars of the Metropolitan Railway, *Mayflower* and *Galatea*, which ran from 1910 to 1939 between Aldgate and the countrified ends of the line in Bucks. Aimed at City gents who wanted to unwind – as a matter of urgency – they were basically cocktail bars on wheels. At the time of writing, I am planning a third trip, this time with champagne, for my son's birthday.

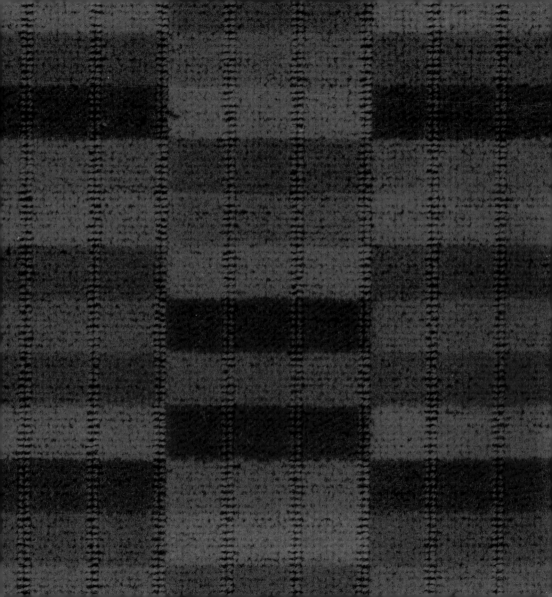

NEW ROUTEMASTER

A friend who knew I was writing this book sent me an email saying he'd just been on a New Routemaster (aka Boris Bus) 'and I realised the moquette extravagance amounts to no fewer than three separate patterns.'

He put this down to 'the blank cheque from Boris', and to many people the bus is, like its commissioner Boris Johnson (when he was Mayor of London), a rather entitled phenomenon. It is arrogantly prolonged, like a Cadillac; it has three doors and two staircases.

Johnson had promised London not only a bus as stylish as the Routemaster, but also a hop-on, hop-off platform (the ability to 'take a risk' as he frankly put it) and a conductor . . . but since the conductors on the New Routemaster didn't take fares, they were like actors playing the part of conductors while keeping an eye on the hopping on and off. The critics also point to the technical troubles: the hybrid diesel-electric engine using

too much diesel; the ineffective cooling system.

Personally, I like the bus. I like the diagonal swirl of the rear window, by which the designer, Thomas Heatherwick, meant to evoke the staircase of the B-Type. I like the wood, or wood effect, on the staircases. Above all, I like the warm colour of the interior, to which the moquette, in burgundy and a mysterious grey/green, makes a big contribution. There are indeed three patterns: a deco-ish vortex on the seat back, another on the seat base (both with massive repeats, meaning they would be expensive to replace), and a check trim on the seat sides.

Speaking of the original Routemaster in its penultimate year (2004), the journalist Andrew Gilligan wrote, 'Sample, while you can . . . an internal colour scheme that does not look like the bottom of a swimming pool.' Thanks to the New Routemaster (I prefer not to call it the Boris Bus) we can do so again.

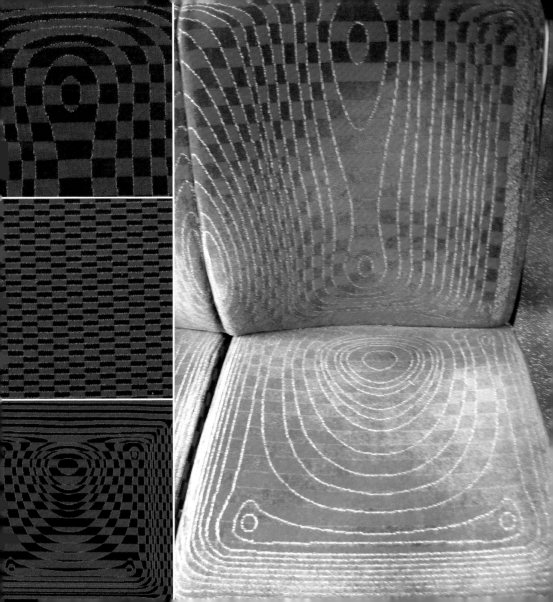

NEW TUBE FOR LONDON

Those who notice – and object to – the oldness of some Tube stocks might like to know that the future will be arriving eventually. It will do so in the form of the New Tube for London (slightly irritating name: who else is it going to be for?), which will bring new trains and signalling to the Piccadilly, Bakerloo, Northern, Central and Waterloo & City Lines from 2023.

The design vision of the new trains was provided by the firm of Priestman Goode, who also designed, for example, the interior of Terminal 5 at Heathrow, and are working on 'about five trains at any one time'. The train will look like a sort of science fiction glow worm, the cab being surrounded by a halo of white light. Illumination will also be important in the interiors: the door surrounds will have lights that change from red to amber to green before they open, so that people will anticipate their opening and so disembark faster, reducing station dwell time.

I read somewhere that this moquette for the

New Tube evoked 'the light trails of vehicles moving at night' – an image of movement. But in an interview for the London Transport Museum Moquette Project, Paul Priestman used an image of stasis: 'Any train is a point in place and time. It conveys a sense of place. Take the Bullet Train in Japan – that's an icon of the country.' When a train achieves that status it becomes, he believes, 'owned by the people, not the designer.'

Priestman sought to give the New Tube a quality of London-ness, and amongst the reference points for the colour of the interior (and of the moquette) were the Oxblood tiles of the Yerkes Tube stations, and the green patina of old Church roofs. The Priestman Goode plans, however, will be subject to modification. The first New Tube was originally intended for the Bakerloo. It will now go onto the Piccadilly, and this moquette will be adapted by an in-house TfL designer, Claire Dilnot-Smith, to reflect the Piccadilly line colour.

BARMAN ON THE BAKERLOO

In 2015, a splodgy blue and red moquette (below) that had replaced Art Deco on the Bakerloo was looking worn out, so Wallace Sewell recoloured Barman for the line, making it grey and charcoal, so that evening appears to have overtaken the landmarks depicted in the pattern, and the orange-red curlicue of the London Eye now earns its colour, since the actual Eye is illuminated in red at night. That red was originally going to be Bakerloo brown (or 'terracotta', as it is officially and more politely called), but the shade looked too drab.

The crepuscular mood of the darkened Barman suits the Bakerloo Line trains which, dating from 1972, are the oldest on the network. You do feel, sometimes, that you are inside a riveted old tin can, but the shape is elegant, the cream panelling is relaxing, and the mixture of transverse and longitudinal seating (these are the last Tube carriages to be so arranged) offers historical interest as well as – for the more transgressive sort of Londoner – one of the last opportunities to put feet up on seats.

It is interesting, by the way, to see how passengers use these transverse benches or mini-sofas. If the outside of the two places is taken, people don't often try to squeeze into the inside (or window) seat, and when the *outside* seat is free, the new arrival sits down with his or her back to the first occupant, rather than sitting side by side with them, which would be more companionable. Another point about the Bakerloo seats: they – together with those on the almost equally venerable Piccadilly trains – have springs inside them.

Paul Marchant, Head of Product Design at TfL, singles this moquette out for particular praise. 'Harriet and Emma were spot-on with that recolouring. It's perfect.'

Still life with moquette pattern

Emilia Cocking's policy is to take the bus rather than the Tube: 'I've always preferred to see where I'm going.'

A freelance photographer and art director, she became interested in the seat moquettes of London buses, which she generally liked. When I told her not everyone at TfL necessarily agreed – that they wanted more standardisation of bus moquettes, but this was not easy to achieve (the buses being privately operated) – she said, in a somewhat incredulous tone, 'You mean they want them all to be the same?'

Tube moquettes, Emilia concedes, are more 'considered', and 'more attention is paid to them,' which seemed to her a good reason to do a project about buses. She called it *On Diversion*.

Her plan was to catch a bus and then, with the moquette in mind, walk the route, acquiring objects along the way, either 'found' or bought from nearby shops. Sometimes she acquired things that reminded her of the moquettes; sometimes it was the other way around.

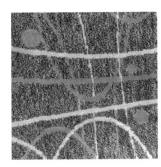

The moquette of the Metroline company, on the 45 (Archway to London Bridge), for example, featured a yellow that reminded her of a hairpiece she'd seen in a shop along the route. She went back and bought it, and combined it with two rolls of red acrylic from an 'arty-crafty' shop in a still life.

The second still life here (she made nine in all) was inspired by the moquette on the 25 (Holborn Circus – Hainault Road), operated by Tower Transit. 'That's certainly the craziest moquette,' she says. She represented it with an astronomical-looking display involving two mothballs, a polystyrene ball, modelling wire and a half-deflated balloon – bathetic items that seem suited to a moquette that doesn't take itself too seriously. But Emilia suggests – rightly, I think – that her compositions amount to 'more than

the sum of their parts', giving 'a living, breathing picture of home.'

emiliacocking.com/ondiversion

TfL RAIL

In 2015, TfL took over Abellio Greater Anglia service between Liverpool Street and Shenfield east of London, and in 2018 it also took over the Heathrow Connect service between Paddington and Heathrow. Both of these lines will be absorbed into Crossrail. The trains running on the Shenfield line were lumbering and boxy old Class 315s – so old they were made in York (where trains haven't been made for a while), and while this antiquated fleet was destined to be replaced by the sleek new Crossrail trains (as much of it already has been), it received a bit of a makeover to acknowledge the change of operator. The new moquette did not have to make any momentous statement. It could be, so to speak, a holding pattern.

Riding along the line between Liverpool Street and Shenfield, the designers, Wallace Sewell, who designed it, photographed (below) 'some sort of generating station or electrical unit – just a shed, really.' But they liked the colour ('greeny blues') and

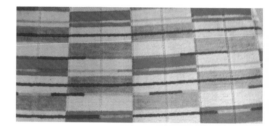

the proportions of the rectangles made by wires or pipes running horizontally across the front of it. This inspired their moquette, which was cheap – as required – but in fact has eight colours, twice the usual amount. 'But it only has two or three colours in any one *line*,' Emma Sewell explained. This is a money-saving weaving trick, the technicalities of which I could not quite grasp. 'It's *very* complicated,' Emma Sewell said, sympathetically (or perhaps pityingly). As with the Croydon Tram, Wallace Sewell also did the Priority moquette here: 'Same colours but playing around.'

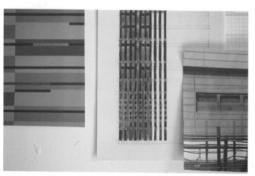

PRIVATE BUS MOQUETTES

Since 1994, London buses have been privately operated but regulated by TfL. Whether they are sufficiently regulated design-wise is rather doubted amongst the more aesthetic people in TfL. The terms of the privatisation did not require the buses to carry on being red. It was up to the operators to weigh almost a century of tradition against the chance to promote their own brands…

Out came the paint pots.

But English Heritage stepped in and, after a garish interlude of chocolate-and-cream Routemasters and more, redness was restored. The garishness endures, however, in the case of many London bus interiors.

In 2011, Ivan Bennett, then a designer for TfL, proposed replacing the various 'meaningless' moquettes of London buses with one that 'captured and was influenced by, London's iconography.' He asked Wallace Sewell to create something based on their geometrical designs for the Overground and the Croydon Tram.

I asked Ivan Bennett whether this moquette would be merely offered to the bus operators or imposed on them. 'It would have been imposed on them,' he said, with some asperity . . . and the conditional tense gives the game away. The moquette (opposite, top) was resisted by the operators, so only samples were ever produced. In 2016 another attempt at a universal London bus moquette would be more successful (see next spread).

This stripy effort was on a Star Rider bus operated out of Holloway Garage by MTL Northern, later bought out by Arriva.

As the LT Museum's website notes, this moquette from a Dennis Caetano bus appears to draw on Inca and Mayan traditions – hardly native (one might add) to Neasden or Bexleyheath.

Stagecoach's moquette combines its corporate colours and logo (the yellow and red bits).

This pleasant green version has to be sought out. Currently it certainly seems to be in evidence on routes 15 and 56.

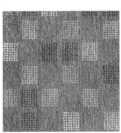

Outside London the entire **Arriva** bus would be painted in these shades of blue.

The **Go-Ahead** group's principal moquette is rather pleasantly reminiscent of houses clustered on a steep hillside at night.

Dutch-owned **Abellio**'s routes tend to be clustered in south-west London.

This less common lilac-based iteration can be found on route 476 in north London.

LONDON BUS

By 2016 the new Mayor of London had put a stop to buying any more New Routemasters. So the bus manufacturers sought to come up with replacements that would retain the best features while dispensing with the eccentricities (like open platforms and three staircases). Wrights, who had built the New Routemaster, came up with the SRM, which stands for Son of Routemaster.

If the New Routemaster was designed late at night over bottles of champagne, the sequel was

created the next morning, in chastened mood with a lot of black coffee. It's elegant rather than flash. The stylish wraparound windscreen and front-end curvature of its predecessor are retained, as is one of the two flamboyant glazed diagonals. Its rear is more vertical and, frankly, more boring than the NR: it does look like 'the back end of a bus'. But the SRM is undoubtedly the second most stylish bus in London.

Alexander Dennis's similarly styled bus,

pictured here, is called a 400 Citybus, and its proper name is the Dennis Enviro, which sounds like a dance-music DJ of the ilk advertised on those mysterious boards taped to lamp-posts – 'Feat. Jazzy Jak with Dennis Enviro'.

These Enviro Citybuses are the most common home of the 2016 London Bus moquette: a second attempt at an official, standardised design for all the capital's buses, commissioned by TfL, though this time the bus operators were not required to use it, and many don't.

Its straightforward check has a pleasing retro feel, in warm red and grey colours obviously descended from the Routemaster line. The privatised array of corporate logos has been supplanted by an understated roundel.

OVERGROUND RECOLOURED

In 2016 the Overground moquette created by Wallace-Sewell in 2008 was re-coloured by a TfL in-house 'innovator' – he prefers that word to 'designer' – called Fernando Solis.

When given the commission, Solis had not been on the Overground. He immediately put that right, and was struck by the quantity of foliage beyond the windows. A moquette, Solis believes, should have a message or a meaning, 'and I knew I wanted to reflect the fact that the line is *overground*, so I brought green into it.' He also introduced 'a dash of yellow', having spotted the small yellow flowers that grew along the line in East London. Asking around about these, he was told they were marigolds, and that people from various cultures along the line throw marigolds on celebratory occasions. The flowers then seed themselves.

As for the orange, he was stuck with that, orange being the line colour. 'Now orange is a weird colour,' he ponders. 'Not many people like orange. To make it work, you have to darken it.' So he did.

The new design was done for the next generation of trains, scheduled for the Gospel Oak-Barking line and those out of Euston and

Liverpool Street, the Class 710s, but delays in bringing them into service meant Solis's moquette has first seen the light of day on the existing trains.

Incidentally, I asked Solis why he preferred 'innovator' to 'designer'. He replied, 'Because design is seen as being merely an accessory, a luxury.'

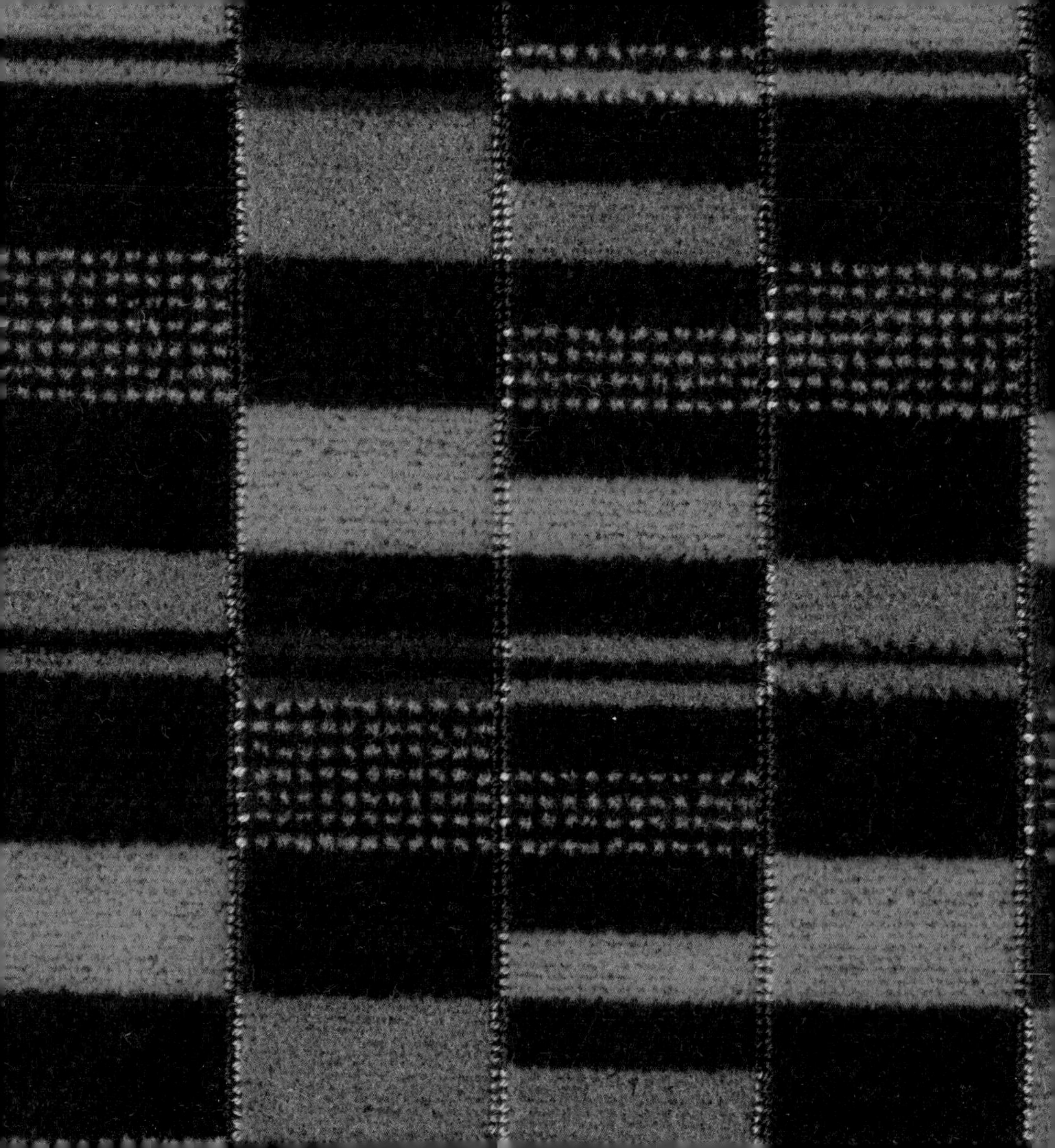

PRIORITY MOQUETTES

The idea of re-arranging a moquette colourway for priority seats comes from TfL. It was first done on London Overground in 2007, when TfL designers re-coloured the original Wallace Sewell design. On Tramlink, Wallace Sewell did it themselves – 'We just mixed around the colours,' says Harriet Wallace-Jones. 'It's like that joke about music: the right notes, not necessarily in the right order.'

But in the years since Tramlink Priority (opposite, bottom) and Crossrail Priority (see p. 186, bottom), there has been a growing suspicion in TfL that something more definite is needed than a mere re-colouring of a main moquette, and on the Jubilee Line a new solution has been attempted.

Until 2019, the priority seats on the Jubilee had been Barman with the 'disabled' pictogram. The TfL designer and innovator Fernando Solis, who had re-coloured Overground Standard, was tasked with creating something better. He doesn't like the pictogram, because many disabilities cannot be shown in that crude manner, including his own. He wanted to create a priority seat reflecting the spirit of the increasingly prevalent legend: 'Not all disabilities are visible'. If this message hits home, then people are less likely to question anyone's right to sit on the priority seat . . . although in my experience people generally neither note nor observe its specialness. They flop down in it if it happens to be free.

Solis felt that the existing priority re-colourings

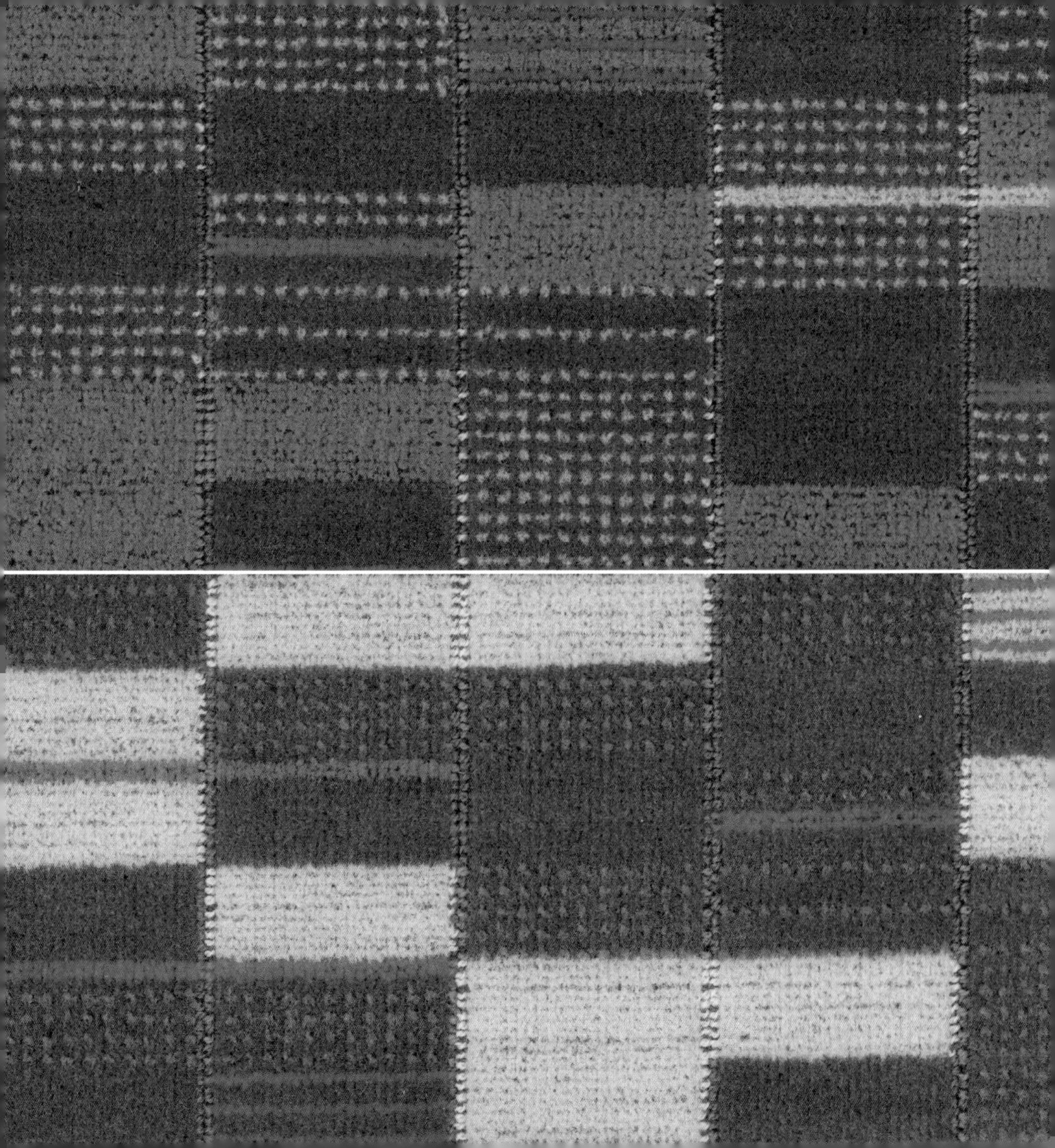

tended to look simply faded, as though that seat had been mysteriously exposed to more sunlight than its neighbours. For the Jubilee he wanted to create a truly 'effective' contrast: one that looked deliberate but was not too divergent from the standard seats. Too much, and the Priority seat might look like 'the naughty child seat'.

So he didn't just juggle the Barman colours, he introduced new ones, determined by their LRV (Light Reflectance Value) number. His new Barman has an elegant grey background and a brighter red ('warning-sign red'), and a new blue ('safety blue', as used on disabled badges). There are also a variety of messages written in circles on the seat backs. One reads, 'Please offer this seat', which ought at least to prick the conscience of the occupant if he or she sees someone more in need of sitting down.

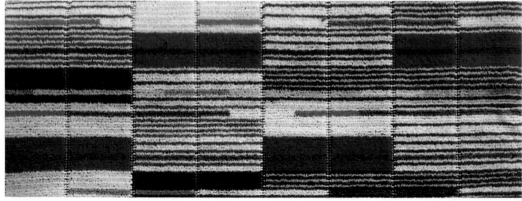

ELIZABETH LINE

The moquette for the new Crossrail trains (the Class 345s, which have been in service since 2017 alongside the old Class 315s on the TfL Rail routes (see pp. 176-7) was originally going to be created by the designer of the trains. But then Wallace Sewell were called in – a justification of the view expressed by most moquette designers, namely that they, and not industrial designers, should be designing the moquettes.

Wallace Sewell were given four weeks to come up with the design – a challenge they relished. The moquette was always going to involve purple, this being the principal colour (other than white) of the trains' exterior. But when it was decided that the line be called the Elizabeth Line (a name no more likely to catch on than 'Baker Street & Waterloo Railway' was in the case of what was immediately and universally known as the Bakerloo Line), the shade was altered to become

a *royal* purple. The design is otherwise inspired by Wallace Sewell's Interim Crossrail moquette (see p. 177). So that earlier design, intended as temporary, is embarking on a glorious afterlife.

The family name of the Class 345s, by the way, is Aventra, it being obligatory for modern train names to end in a vowel.

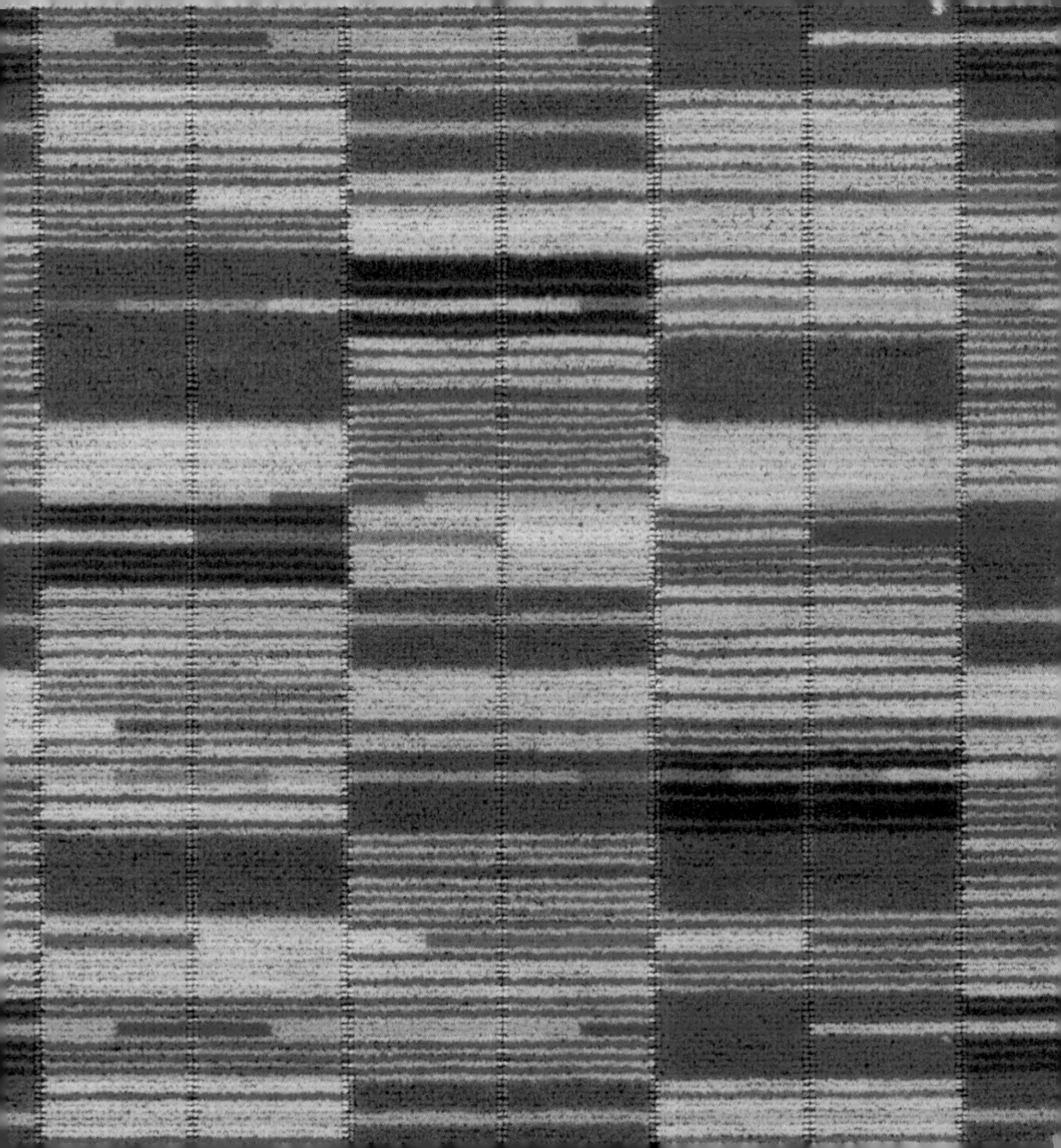

Where can you still sit on vintage moquette?

RT

The Epping-Ongar stretch of the Central Line, which closed in 1994, had been a steam railway

before LT took it over. It is now one again. But because its trains aren't allowed to run into Epping Station, passengers have to catch a vintage bus from there to North Weald in order to board the steam train. I say 'have to', but the bus ride is a delight, and you might find yourself sitting on the brown moquette of an RT, or something equally dashing.

1938 RETRIM

Two 1938 Stock Tube trains have been preserved: one by the London Transport Museum and one, which ran the final journey on the Epping-Ongar line when it closed in 1994, by a group called Cravens Heritage Trains. Both are still brought out on occasion for special tours of part of the Underground network – though as new signalling comes in the number of lines where they can go

is diminishing. The interiors carry the rich red-and-green check used to refurbish the 1938 stock in the Seventies.

ROUTEMASTER

As every engaged couple discover, a wedding brings an overwhelming list of Things to Do. Date, venue, menu, and we nearly forgot table napkins! It being compulsory these days to make your dressed-up-to-the-nines guests travel to the reception on an old Routemaster, it is still easy to overlook the most important thing of all about getting married: the correct moquette on your bus.

For the most important day of your life Poached Egg/Eyes Down/Crushed Strawberry is

and longitudinal seats, the guard could throw no light on when the Metropolitan Diamonds appeared. 'Think it's always been there,' he shrugged. The old green has been banished from the interior, but since it was meant to remind Londoners of the countryside, perhaps it's not required when running through real countryside.

The trains retain their external red, but there is some sign of corrosion by sea spray: not a fate any London Underground train could reasonably have anticipated.

not on. You need classic Routemaster. Several heritage fleets, like Ensignbus or Redroutemaster, can provide it, but only on certain vehicles. With the former RM25 will do, but definitely *not* RML 2734.

METROPOLITAN DIAMONDS

In the mid-1960s, the surviving railway line on the Isle of Wight was raised at the Ryde end to prevent seawater flooding, which meant only London Tube trains could now fit through the tunnel to the south.

When I rode these ancient 1938 Stock trains, with their wooden window ledges, transverse

Index